WORKJOBS II

NUMBER ACTIVITIES
FOR EARLY CHILDHOOD

MARY BARATTA-LORTON

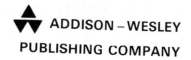 ADDISON – WESLEY
PUBLISHING COMPANY

Menlo Park, California • Reading, Massachusetts
London • Amsterdam • Don Mills, Ontario • Sydney

Acknowledgments

Special thanks to Sunnyslope School, Nick Ferrero, principal (Hollister, CA) and Ohlone School, James Mathiott, principal (Palo Alto, CA) where all the photographs were taken.

Teachers: Diane Campbell-Howard, Helen Fleming, Susan Stevlingson

Children

Jo-Ann Bailon
Tano Bailon
Angelique Barboa
Michael Berkowitz
Ronnie Bland
Megan Bowles
Tobin Brockett
Mike Brown
Albert Correa
Chet Di Lauro
Wendy Dolfin
Simeon Flick
Rebecca Folsom
Jamie Ghione
Connie Gibson
Debbie Gibson
Justino Gómez
Brian Gong

Victor Gonzalez
Kelley Hayashi
Natalie Hegg
Kurt Heiner
Norma Hernandez
Sandy Hernandez
Treny Hernandez
Peter Hitchcock
Tracy Kirkpatrick
John Klauer
Scott Leonard
Richard Luwecka
Jamie Maddux
Cherylle Magno
Susannah Manley
Carrie Ellen Mathiott
Richelle Mattish
Ricky Mattish
Shannan McDermott

Amy McGuire
Tim McMorrow
Devin McOsker
Leopoldo Miranda
Doreen Moss
Lisa Mueller
Stephen Muller
Natasha Newson
Valerie Nichols
Rodney Noble
Gina Norris
Lisa Norris
Kim O'Brien
Gerardo Ochoa
Angelina Ortega
Catalina Ortiz
Maribel Parawan
Kristie Paterson
Jenny Pattisson

Melissa Rabello
Irma Adriano Reynoso
Bonnie Ripley
Beanna Rodriguez
Renee Ruvalcaba
Erik Sabot
Pat Salcedo
Todd Smith
Sean Stanley
Jonathan Sweeten
Tina Tabancay
Tony Torquato
Albert Valles, Jr.
Jason Vanclef
Barry Waldron
Tonya Watts
John Williams
Kristi Woodall
Lisa Yacavon

For help and support above and beyond the call of duty, thank you:

Bob Baratta-Lorton and the staff of the Center for Innovation in Education
All the teachers who have made Workjobs for the children in their classes
Vivian Bailon
Kathy Richardson and Marilyn Burns for editorial suggestions
Beatrice Baratta, Robin Huber, Cappy Springer, and Kris Nelson for typing and retyping

Photography: John Madden, Geri Madden, Palo Alto, CA

Art Work: Robert A. Larsen, Cupertino, CA

Design: Wendy Palmer and the staff of Reprographex, Palo Alto, CA

Royalties from this book accrue to the Center for Innovation in Education to support innovative activities in education for both children and teachers.

How to Quickly Familiarize Yourself With Workjobs II

1. Read pages 2 and 3.
2. Glance at each title in the Table of Contents.
3. Read page 6 and then quickly skan pages 7–20.
4. Flip through pages 40–91 being careful not to miss the green inserted card.
5. Read pages 122–124.

WORKJOBS II

early childhood

Table of Contents

Part IV   Presenting the Activities

Part V   Appendix

PART I

Introduction

What Is a Workjob?

A Workjob is simply a manipulative activity using familiar concrete materials from the child's world that is designed to be completed in about ten minutes by a kindergarten, first or second grade student. It requires a specific action from the child and it is through this action that the child develops a new understanding of the given concept.

During my early years of teaching I made many of these independent activity-centered games for the children in my class to use. During one of these years the word "workjob" was coined by a student of mine named Leretha, who took one of the "jobs", as I called them, over to a corner and could be heard saying aloud over and over, "Work, work, work, work, work." An older child, working as a tutor and wanting to be sure, I suppose, that Leretha was sticking to business, asked, "Are you doing your job?" Leretha looked up indignantly and said, "Can't you see I'm doing my workjob?" Other children picked up on this and pretty soon it was standard vocabulary in our classroom. Every time I said, "Go and choose a job to do," the children said, "Oh, I want the 'go-together' workjob," or some such thing. Eventually I gave in and used the phrase too. Ultimately these activities were published in a book called WORKJOBS.

What Is WORKJOBS II?

WORKJOBS II was written to provide kindergarten, first and second grade teachers with complete instructions for making and using twenty open-ended math activities as an enriching supplement to their present classroom math program. In this program the children have many opportunities to use child-oriented counters and gameboards to explore the concept of number from counting to making up and solving their own addition and subtraction equations.

Through the use of these materials the children have an opportunity to explore the many facets of each number and the various relationships that exist between numbers. The teacher becomes more aware of the developmental levels which the child passes through in acquiring a full, flexible understanding of the concept of number.

How Does a WORKJOBS II Activity Differ from an Original Workjob?

When I started teaching first and second grade after having taught kindergarten for several years, I found many of my original Workjobs could be changed to make them more appropriate for the greater developmental range. I took all the numerals off the mathematics Workjobs and made them more open-ended. (I just covered the numerals with gummed labels.) This enabled me to specify how an individual child was to use the activity and thereby provide whatever level was appropriate. A child could put numeral cards with the activities in October, equation cards with them in January, and perhaps write his or her own problems for the same activity in March.

I also found I needed more activities with essentially the same concept in order to provide repetitive practice without having it seem repetitious to the children. By making many varied activities, seemingly different, but alike in usage, I avoided having to explain "what to do" with each different activity. Once the children understood that each activity had counters and an area on which to place them, it didn't matter what the actual counters or counting areas were; the procedure for all the activities was understood. This greatly reduced introduction time as well as individual explanations. All my attention could now be focused on stimulating conceptual development, asking questions, and guiding the growth of the children's social skills rather than on explaining procedure. I found this to be a much more suitable and rewarding use of my time and energy as a teacher.

Which Mathematical Skills Are Developed?

Counting

1:1 Correspondence

Numeral Form

Numeral Recognition

Conservation of Number

Relationships Within and Between Numbers

The Process of Addition

The Process of Subtraction

Interpreting Symbols

Writing and Solving Addition and Subtraction Equations

Use of WORKJOBS II with Other Math Programs

WORKJOBS II is designed to supplement whatever program teachers are using. It provides a link between the child's world (the twenty concrete, child-centered activities) and the adult's world (the mathematical symbols and abstractions); WORKJOBS II forms a bridge that begins at the child's concrete, material level and leads the child to this adult world of abstraction.

These twenty WORKJOBS II activities and the program utilizing them can supplement any existing mathematics program in a kindergarten, first or second grade classroom. It deals only with the arithmetic strand, though, so concepts such as patterning, sorting and classification, measurement, shapes, problem solving and place value need to be fully developed in some other way to round out each child's mathematical understanding.

Many teachers may be familiar with my earlier book MATHEMATICS *THEIR* WAY, and may be curious about the relationship between this program and WORKJOBS II. Teachers using MATHEMATICS *THEIR* WAY as full math programs would teach from Chapters 1–7 to develop the concepts of free exploration, pattern, sorting, counting, comparing, graphing and number. This is done through total class participation, and small group work. WORKJOBS II would then supplement Chapters 8 and 9 (Number at the Connecting and Symbolic Levels). The WORKJOBS II activities can be used at this stage to enable half the class to work independently while the other half works with the teacher on a directed lesson selected from Chapters 8–12 (Number At the Connecting Level, Number At The Symbolic Level, Pattern II, Place Value, Pattern Book Experiments).

PART II

A Look Ahead

An Overview of the Activities

Activity-centered learning is a valuable approach because it utilizes the child's natural style of learning, allowing the child to develop concepts from the actual manipulation of the environment. The child can be helped to move gradually from a "hands on" experience to ever-increasing levels of abstraction and symbolism.

In using Workjobs, ideally, each child uses the activities to explore number cycling from lesser to greater abstraction. Beginning with concrete experiences, the child is gradually led to more symbolic ones.

After a few weeks in a typical kindergarten, first or second grade classroom of thirty or more children, students should be working at their appropriate level (determined by the assessment on page 95) side-by-side with children working at other levels—as opposed to working with children at the same level. (Second grade children move toward greater abstraction at a quicker pace than do kindergarten or first grade students, which is quite natural at this age level.)

The first level (the Concept Level) allows a child to confront number and all its various relationships as represented by different concrete materials. This stage can be thought of as intuitive.

The second level (the Connecting Level) attempts to link the concept of number as represented concretely in the familiar materials with the traditional mathematical symbols.

The third level (the Symbolic Level) gives the children an opportunity to express their mathematical thinking in their own handwritten work, and thereby grow to feel at ease with abstraction.

Each of the three levels represents *different types of thinking* almost more than different levels or sequential steps. Potentially, they could be experienced in any order and still produce the same end results, but the three levels are a helpful sequence and structure which guarantees success for all learners.

It is important to remember that children learn in a geometric fashion, not a linear one. A three-year-old will sometimes use remarkably advanced vocabulary years before it would be expected to appear as a natural part of the child's language. A lock-step approach to language development with "mastery tests" for advancement never produces such wonderfully rich, out-of-order progress!

You should get a feel for the three levels by reading the rest of this chapter and looking carefully at the sequence of pictures; but make a conscious effort to prevent your thinking from getting locked into the steps. Children who skip around actually learn more than children forced through each level step-by-step with "proof of mastery" demanded of them before being allowed to progress to the next level. Such a rigid approach would be completely inappropriate here, but it is helpful for a teacher to have a clear understanding of the different types of thinking and uniquely different focus represented by each level. With this understanding, the teacher will be more sensitive to and aware of the experiences which are appropriate for individual children at particular stages of development and thereby guide the children more skillfully.

A Photographic Collage
of the Developmental Levels

A child could explore the numbers from 0–9 with the 20 activities at each of the three separate levels (Concept, Connecting and Symbolic), and then explore the operations of addition and subtraction, again, at these same three levels. This is a six-fold recycling of each Workjob activity.

Mathematical Concept	Developmental Level
Exploring the Numbers 0–9	Concept Level
Exploring the Numbers 0–9	Connecting Level
Exploring the Numbers 0–9	Symbolic Level
Exploring the operations of addition and subtraction	Concept Level
Exploring the operations of addition and subtraction	Connecting Level
Exploring the operations of addition and subtraction	Symbolic Level

The Connecting Level bridges the familiar concrete experience of the child's world to the adult world of abstract symbols.

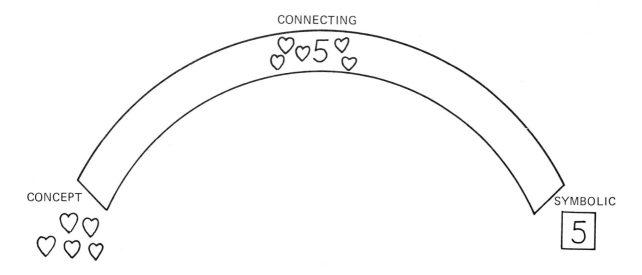

The pictures on the following pages show children at work at each of these different levels, moving from lesser to greater abstraction.

This overview is intended to help you visualize each of the different levels as they would occur in your classroom.

Exploring the numbers from 0–9 at the Concept Level: The children count out the same number of objects onto each counting area.

"One, two, three, four. One, two, three, four. One, two, three, four. One. . . ."

". . . five, six, seven, eight. One, two, three, four, five, six, seven, eight. One. . . ."

". . . five, six, seven. One, two, three, four, five, six, seven. One, two. . . ."

".. . six. One, two, three, four, five, six. One, two. . . ."

".. . four, five. One, two, three, four, five. One, two, three, four, five. One, two. . . ."

"One, two, three. One, two, three. One, two, three. One, two, three. . . ."

Exploring the numbers from 0–9 at the Connecting Level: The children count out the appropriate numbers of counters to match each numeral.

Exploring the numbers from 0–9 at the Symbolic Level: The children record the total number of objects on each counting area on a tiny piece of paper.

Exploring the operation of addition at the Concept Level: The children take turns in pairs verbalizing the combinations created on a counting area—no totals are given at this stage.

"We went to the pet store and bought one fish for our new tank."

"Then we bought five more."   "That's one and five."

"Its your turn now. I went fishing with my Uncle Bill. We could see six fish in the pool."

"Four more swam in . . . six and four."

Exploring the operation of subtraction at the Concept Level: The children take turns playing a "take away" game verbalizing the process of subtraction to their partner—no remainders are given at this stage.

"Mama bird laid four baby bird eggs."

"One egg fell out of the nest by accident . . . four minus one."

"It's my turn now. My nest has five eggs in it. If I take out three of them, that's five minus three."

Exploring the operation of addition at the Connecting Level: The children use counters representing each equation concretely.

Exploring the operation of subtraction at the Connecting Level: The children use counters representing each equation concretely.

Exploring the operation of addition at the Symbolic Level: The children build an addition problem from an equation card, recording the combination and total on a separate piece of paper.

Exploring the operation of addition at the Symbolic Level: The children use a numeral card to indicate the total number of objects to be used on each counting area. After building this number with their objects the children record the combination and total on a separate piece of paper.

Exploring the operation of subtraction at the Symbolic Level: The children build a subtraction problem from an equation card, recording the process and remainder on a separate piece of paper.

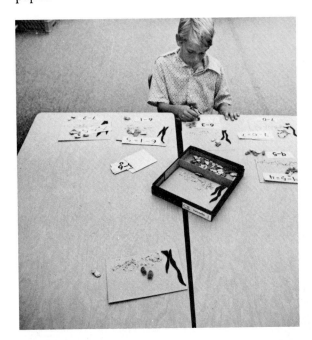

Exploring the operation of subtraction at the Symbolic Level: The children use a numeral card to indicate the total they will build on each counting area. They subtract whatever amount they wish and then record both the subtraction process and the remainder on a separate piece of paper.

Prerequisite Skills

In order for children to benefit fully from WORKJOBS II they need to have sufficient skill with 1:1 correspondence to comfortably count out four objects.

Children will eventually need to *write* the numbers and, consequently, need to begin activities to develop this skill months before they need to have acquired it.

COUNTING TO FOUR

A child who cannot count four objects confidently and consistently needs to do the following series of lessons before using the Workjobs.

Give the child thirty squares of tagboard and some wooden cubes. Ask the child to put two cubes on each paper. If this is easily accomplished, the next day ask

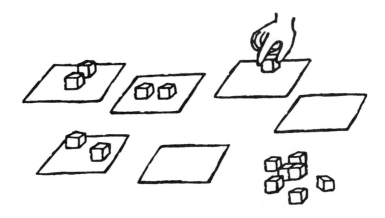

the child to put three blocks on each. If this is difficult (e.g., the child puts one cube or two cubes on some squares rather than consistently putting three), the teacher should put two dots on each square of tagboard after school, using a black crayon (a felt tip pen bleeds through to the other side).

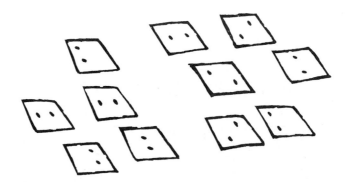

The next day the child matches the cubes to the dots, guaranteeing success.

If matching cubes to the two dots is easy, the following day the child should be asked to put out the squares with the dotted sides face down, and again to try to put two cubes on each square. If this is easy, the teacher can add one more dot to each tagboard square after school; the next day the child will match three cubes to the three dots on each piece of tagboard.

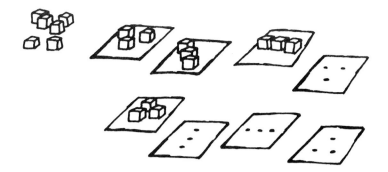

When this seems easy, ask the child to put three cubes on the plain side of the tagboard. If this is too hard, the child can turn the cards over, one at a time, match the cubes to the dots, then remove the blocks, turn the card back over and place three blocks on the plain side.

When the child comfortably and successfully counts out three blocks onto the plain side of the squares three consecutive times, the teacher can add another dot to the cards and ask the child to put down groups of four cubes. Once this is accomplished, the child is ready to begin using the WORKJOBS II activities as described in Part IV.

NUMERAL FORM

During the first two weeks of school the teacher will want to assess every child in class (kindergarten, first and second grade) for correct numeral form. It is helpful and interesting to have this early information with which to make later comparisons.

The teacher should cut ten 3″ × 5″ pieces of tagboard and write one number (0,1,2,3,4,5,6,7,8 or 9) on each card with a black marking pen.

Three children at a time are asked to go to the chalkboard while the rest of the class works on a variety of independent activities which require no adult supervision (drawing, looking at books, etc.). The teacher says to the three children at the chalkboard, "Show me how you write a number five." The teacher holds up a card for them to see with the number five written on it. (If the teacher fails to show the number, visual memory as well as numeral form is being tested and you can't isolate accurately one skill from the other.)

The teacher should pay close attention to the strokes each child makes to form each number. The numbers from zero to nine are given one at a time out of order. The teacher may ask the children to make a second number to double check a child she or he is unsure of or who was missed. This is a good check on an individual child's consistency with the correct form.

A number made skillfully will be flowing and effortless. Keep a record of any numbers which were made facing the wrong direction (reversed), or from incorrect position (starting from the bottom rather than the top), or with great hesitation and effort.

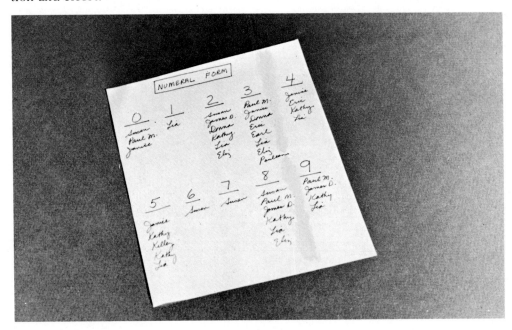

Once the teacher knows which children need practice and help with which numbers, this needed practice can begin.

THE THEORY BEHIND THE PURPLE-GREEN SYSTEM

The goal is for each child to internalize the starting position, order and direction of the strokes or parts that combine to form the numerals. By practicing these strokes, the child will also strengthen the small muscles which are used in writing.

If the order of the strokes of each number is analyzed and the teacher writes the first stroke in one color and the second stroke in a second color, the child quickly learns the pattern and can work independently learning to make all the numbers correctly and smoothly (letters and shapes, too, if desired).

Having a consistent color pattern or sequence to rely on, the child no longer must reinvent or memorize the process, thinking "How do I make that?" or

"Where do I start?" or "Which direction do I go?". The child's practice is more effective since every time the child makes the strokes they are in the same order. This reinforces the correct pattern and helps the child internalize the most efficient way of writing each numeral.

The teacher makes a large numeral in front of the children every few days using a purple crayon for the first stroke and a green crayon for the second. (These particular colors were chosen because they are easily distinguishable and are both available as ditto masters for readily preparing related classroom materials.)

The children practice all the numbers by tracing them four times: in the air, on their palms, on one another's backs and on their individual chalkboards.*

While tracing the number in the air and in the palms of their hands the children say the name of the color with which each stroke is made, not the name of the number. This helps the children internalize the pattern; it is not the point of the lesson to learn the names of the numbers.

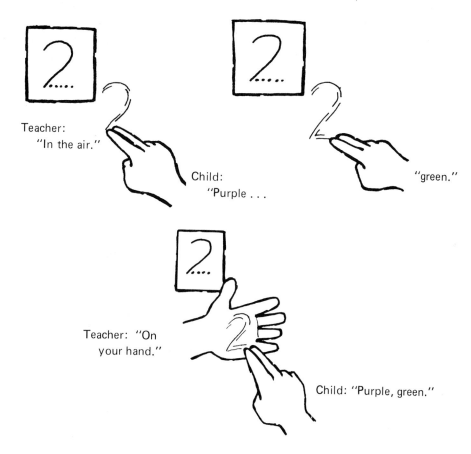

Teacher: "In the air."
Child: "Purple . . . "green."
Teacher: "On your hand."
Child: "Purple, green."

This helps the children internalize the pattern; it is not the point of the lesson to learn the names of the numbers.

*Individual chalkboards can be easily made by painting pieces of heavy chipboard (with a brush, not spray), using slate paint or chalkboard paint, available in all large hardware stores. Ask the children to bring an old sock from home which becomes the eraser and holder for their chalk. *Buy chalk at the dime store to use; school chalk has a hardener added to make it dustless and will scratch the boards.*

The children should trace each number three times in the air and three times in the palms of their hands, each time repeating the colors:

Teacher: "In the air."
Children: "Purple, green, purple, green, purple, green."

Teacher: "On your hand."
Children: "Purple, green, purple, green, purple, green."

Now the children turn and trace the number on one another's backs three times, saying the name of the number rather than the colors.

The teacher should check carefully to be sure all the children have the pattern internalized before directing them to say the number names instead of the colors. Saying the colors reinforces the pattern. Saying the number names assumes the child consistently uses the internalized pattern and is ready for another step.

The final step is for the children to *write* the number several times on their individual chalkboards.

INDIVIDUALIZED NUMBER PRACTICE

The teacher groups together the children who need help on a certain number for a lesson.

The children who need help writing numbers other than the one presently being worked on should work on individualized number practice activities.*

Number line templates in purple and green†

Gluing down black yarn one stroke at a time ‡

Numeral sequence cards in purple and green†

Dot to Dots; Numbers in purple and green†

Gluing down macaroni‡

Writing papers in purple and green*

*Look for ideas under "Learning to Write Numerals" on pages 43–51 in MATHEMATICS *THEIR* WAY.

†Available at cost from The Center for Innovation in Education, 19225 Vineyard Lane, Saratoga, CA 95070.

‡See Appendix, pages 125–132. Run on tagboard when using macaroni and on paper when using yarn.

It is imperative that the teacher clearly understand that the purpose of the purple and green pattern is to be a teaching tool or guide. It is made available to the child only as a sequencing reference. It is never to be copied with purple and green colors when actually writing. The child writes in black with a crayon, pen or pencil, *never* with the purple and green colors. This mistaken procedure would actually distract the child's attention from the sequential pattern.

ADVANCED NUMBER PRACTICE

Children who know how to write all the numbers benefit nonetheless from a five- to six-minute review lesson with all their classmates once a week. The rest of the time they should be asked to do one of the following activities independently while the rest of the class works on the numbers they need to practice, either independently or in the teacher-directed group.

1. Dice Graph

   Materials: Dotted dice or wooden cubes with 0,1,2,3,4,5 dots (made with a permanent marking pen)
   Dittoed graph paper

   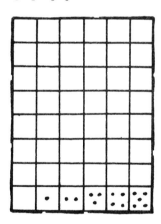

   The child shakes one die and records the number rolled above the appropriate dot pattern. When one column reaches the top of the graph the child stops.

When interest in making individual records wanes have several children work together adding to a huge piece of graph paper.

2. Number Sequences

   Materials: Each group of four or five children needs ten wooden cubes with numbers written on the faces (five dice with numbers zero to five and five dice with numbers four to nine)
   Paper and pencils

One child in a small group of children shakes the ten dice.

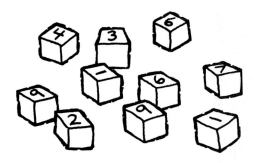

Everyone works to arrange the dice in as many pairs and sequences as possible.

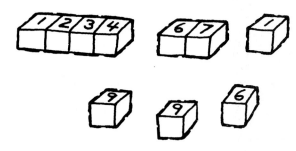

When finished, the children record the sequences made on their paper.

The children in the group take turns rolling the ten dice. They record each resulting number sequence on their paper. Previously rolled sequences are tallied and new sequences are added to the lists.

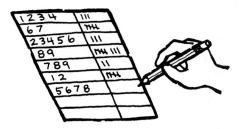

3. Repeating Number Patterns

Materials: A three foot sheet of butcher paper, rolled up and cut to two inches wide
Pencils and crayons

The teacher begins a repeating number pattern on the chalkboard such as 133813381338. The children predict the next five or six numbers verbally, and then begin working on their own.

Each day a new pattern can be started.

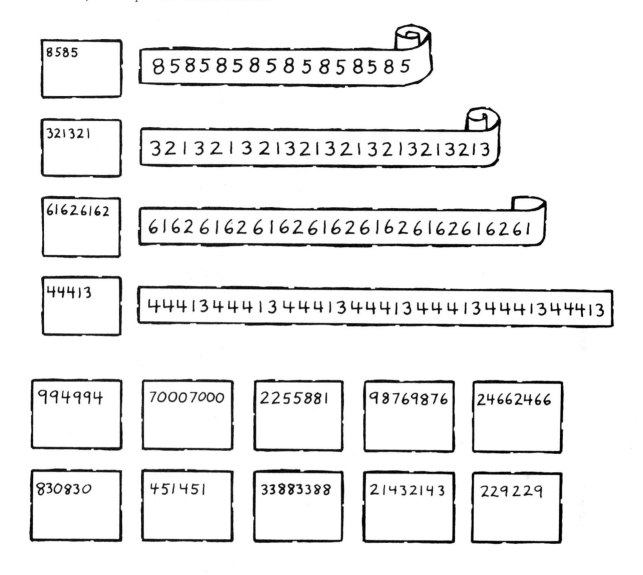

The teacher should be careful to balance over time the inclusion of each number from zero to nine in the various patterns. Very soon the children can be encouraged to make up patterns for one another.

Another variation of writing patterns is to have two or three children work together to make one four-inch strip. The paper is laid out on the floor and each child takes a turn writing one number. It is actually more difficult to add a part of a part to a pattern rather than repeating the entire part, which makes this in effect a completely different activity.

PART III

Descriptions and Directions
for Making the Activities

The Structure of the Activities

Each activity has two components: 80–100 counters and something into or onto which the counters are placed. The counters and counting areas for the twenty activities are as follows:

Counters	Counting Areas
1. fish	aquariums
2. eggs	nests
3. lights	pine trees
4. pins	pincushions
5. corn	chicken gameboards
6. cookies	plates
7. airplanes	airport runway gameboards
8. watermelon seeds	watermelon slices
9. pumpkins and ghosts	haunted house gameboards
10. spaghetti and meatballs	place-setting gameboards
11. mice	mousetraps
12. apples	buckets
13. leaves	trees
14. strawberries	strawberry patch gameboards
15. frogs and toads	ponds
16. bacon and eggs	plates
17. men's and women's faces	snapshots gameboards
18. candles	birthday cake gameboards
19. rocks	river gameboards
20. shells	sandy beaches

Each of the activities is designed in one of two ways: 1) with one kind of counter and *two* parts to the counting area, or 2) with two kinds of counters and only *one* part to the counting area. Both organizational techniques enable the child to naturally create and thereby discover the various combinations and relationships within each number explored.

The organization for the twenty activities are of both these types:

Organizational Scheme A

One kind of counter on a divided counting area.

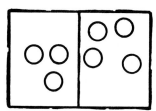

beaded pins	two-tone pincushion
corn	two-part chicken game-board
airplanes	divided runway game-board
rocks	divided river
shells	on the beaches and in the ocean game-boards

Organizational Scheme B

Two colors or kinds of counters on an undivided counting area.

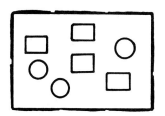

two colors of fish	aquarium
two colors of eggs	nest
two colors of lights	pine tree
chocolate and vanilla cookies	plate
black and white seeds	watermelon slice
ghosts and pumpkins	haunted house
spaghetti and meat-balls	place setting gameboard
pink-eared and black-eared mice	mousetrap
red and green apples	bucket
light and dark leaves	tree game-board
ripe and unripe strawberries	strawberry patch
frogs and toads	pond
bacon and eggs	plate
men's and women's faces	snapshots gameboard
two colors of candles	birthday cake gameboard

When creating your own ideas for open-ended mathematics Workjobs, this structure will help guide you. If you can find a counter you would like to use, think:

1. "What could this be used with in real life that would have two parts?" (which would give you a divided counting area) or;

2. "What else would naturally be found along with this?" (to give you two kinds of counters) and then, "In what kind of life setting would these two objects be found together?" (this gives you a counting area).

You might use red and yellow plastic flowers in a milk carton vase, or cut flowers from yellow felt to place on two grassy fields (light and dark green felt). You might put little boats on two blue felt ocean waves, or put sailboats and row boats on a blue felt ocean. You might park tiny cars in two, side-by-side parking lots, or have cars and bicycles in one lot. You could have blue and red buttons to place on felt or pelon shirt cut-outs or white buttons for dresses and pants. You could put pennies in a partitioned piggy bank, or pennies and centavos in one undivided piggy bank. It's fun! Just look around and use your imagination.

Why These Particular Twenty Activities Are Suggested

I made and used many, many different activities in my classroom before I settled on the ones described in this book to share with you. These activities survived for good reasons:
1. The materials have proved to be durable.
2. They are relatively easy and inexpensive to assemble.
3. They are made with common, familiar materials from the child's environment.
4. Young children are naturally attracted to these materials and maintain their interest in using them over time. This natural motivation makes the activities enjoyable while at the same time provides young children a series of meaningful learning experiences.

Rationale for the Number of Counters and Counting Areas Included in Each Workjob

Each activity has eight counting areas and between eighty and one hundred counters. I originally put ten counting areas with each activity, as I'm sure seems initially more reasonable to you. I learned about the children's attitude toward this quite by accident.

In the middle of the year I lent two teachers some of the counting areas as models for games they wanted to duplicate. These teachers were from out of town so it was about ten days before the counting areas were returned through the mail. During those ten days several of the Workjobs were short two of their ten counting areas. I hesitated to leave them on the shelf, but I did. During these ten days I gradually realized that the children seemed to be developing a preference for these activities. I began to piece things together and watched more closely to see what was happening. The children who always worked slowly and with such a struggle and those who often needed encouragement from an adult in order to finish their work, seemed changed. I was surprised to find some of these children finishing two activities in the time it previously took them to do one. There was also a difference in their attitudes while working as well as when they finished.

What I think I stumbled on was the appropriate length of time for young children to work at one sitting. For these activities eight seemed to be a magic number. I tried to put myself in the place of the children for whom it seemed to make such a difference. I then could imagine how working with eight gameboards rather than ten might seem less overwhelming and give me the feeling that I can do it. Ten might be more than I could picture doing with ease, giving me the feeling of endless work.

As an experiment, I removed two counting areas from all the games and there was a change in my whole class; it seemed that eight was good for everyone, not just for the children who struggle. So, the class seemed more lively, more enthusiastic, more inner directed, and seemed to get even more work accomplished, more joyfully. It is for this reason that eight counting areas are included for each Workjob.

Special Notes on Making the Activities

COUNTERS

There should be from 80–100 counters in each of the twenty activities, but there is no need to have any specific amount. The teacher should feel confident to make whatever number of counters (green felt leaves, meatballs, ghosts, strawberries, etc.) that the suggested amount of supplies will naturally produce.

SEPARATOR STRIPS

Each storage box (except the one containing the airport activity) will be divided into two parts by a strip of cardboard. This is glued into the bottom of the box to provide a separate area for the gameboards and counters. Separator strip:

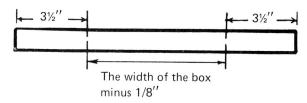

HOW TO PREVENT SPILLS WHEN THE BOXES ARE DROPPED

You will need 20 (4″ long) heavy duty rubber bands or some round elastic from the dime store cut into 9″ lengths and tied with a square knot, scissors, 20 paper clips and a roll of masking tape.

Poke a hole in the top of a WORKJOBS II storage box with the point of your scissors. Push half of the rubber band through the hole and attach a paper clip to the rubber band on the inside of the lid. Pull from the outside so the paper clip is tight against the inside of the lid.

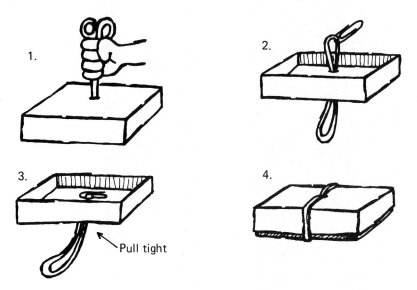

1.

2.

3.

Pull tight

4.

Cover the paper clip on the inside of the lid with a piece of masking tape. All of the rubber band remains on the top of the box and is now ready to be stretched around the outside of the box. This holds the box closed (even when it is dropped) and will prevent the corn, fish or shells from spilling all over the floor.

The rubber band is attached to the top of the box so it is always visible to the children insuring they will see it and remember to use it. (We used to put it on the bottom of the box to keep the top perfect but the children forgot to use it half the time.)

The purpose of the paper clip is to add strength to the lid and prevent the band from slipping back through the hole.

LABELING THE WORKJOBS STORAGE BOXES

On pages 133 and 135 in the appendix there are two pages of labels which you can use to label two opposite ends of each storage box. With both ends labeled the boxes are always put away so that a labeled end is showing.

 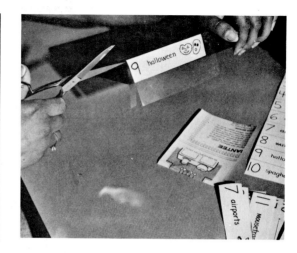

COLORING THE GAMEBOARDS

The masters for the gameboards are on pages 143–146. You will need to make a Thermofax master and run off eight copies of each on heavy tagboard.

It is important that you not overdo the actual coloring of the gameboards. The gameboards are a background for the counters and should not compete with them for the child's attention. Simply color them quickly and lightly with crayon (spend 1–2 minutes per gameboard) and then cover them with clear contact paper.

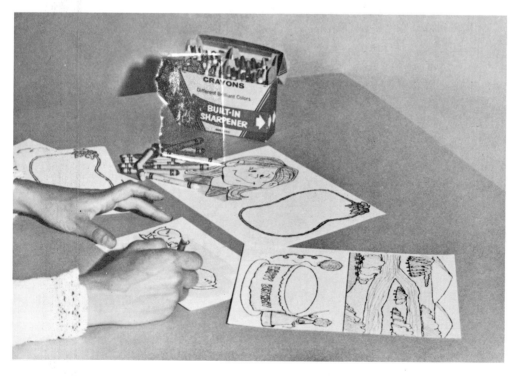

AQUARIUMS

Activity

The child sets out various quantities or creates problems by filling the aquarium with yellow and orange fish, forming various combinations.

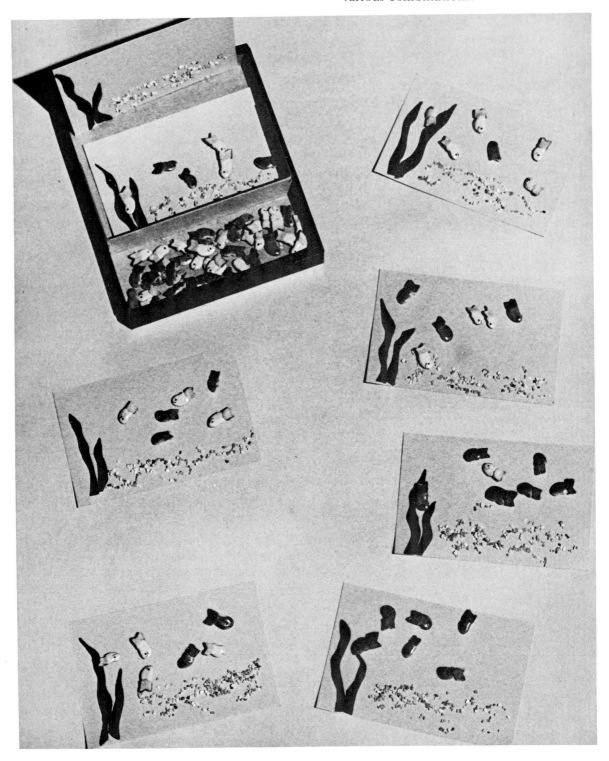

Materials

Storage Container

Storage box (approximately 9″ × 10″ × 1½″)

Separator strip of heavy cardboard (see page 37)

Counting Areas

Eight pieces of light blue railroad board 5½″ × 8½″

1/8 cup of natural aquarium gravel

Light and dark green scraps of felt

White glue

Scissors

Making Directions

Label the opposite ends of a storage box "Fish and Aquariums."

Glue separator strip inside on the bottom of the storage box.

Cut some "water plants" from light and dark green felt scraps and glue two or three on each piece of railroad board.

Dot a few places on each piece of railroad board with white glue. Using the lid from the storage box as a catcher for excess gravel, place the gameboards one at a time in the lid and pour gravel over the glue. Shake off excess gravel and allow to dry thoroughly.

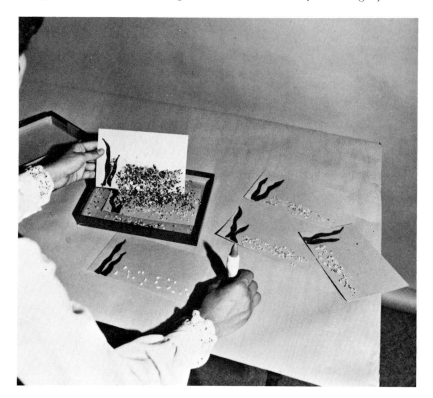

Place the eight aquarium gameboards in the storage box.

Counters

Two pieces of 4″ × 12″ felt (yellow and orange)

3/4 cup large lima beans

Two cans of quick-drying spray paint (orange and yellow)

Newspapers

Black fine line permanent ink marking pen*

Scissors

Cut the 4″ × 12″ pieces of both yellow and orange felt into 1/2″ strips and then into eight "fish-tail" shapes.

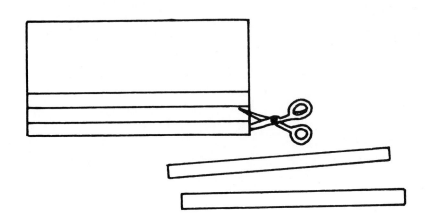

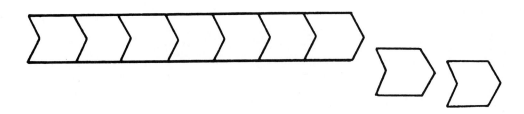

Spread out "several thicknesses of old newspapers"** and put all the large lima beans in the center. They should be as close as possible without actually touching each other. Be sure the paper extends two feet past the beans in every direction to catch the paint's overspray or mist.

Spray paint one side of the beans yellow. Hold the can perpendicular to the beans, not at an angle, so the spray is directed straight down and can't get under the beans.

---

*A "Sharpie" by Sanford is a fine-line permanent ink pen which works well. They are available in stationery and office supply stores. Laundry markers are also excellent.

**Credit for this quote goes to my mom, Beatrice Baratta, who must have said these very words to me a hundred times when I was young . . . usually when it was already too late!

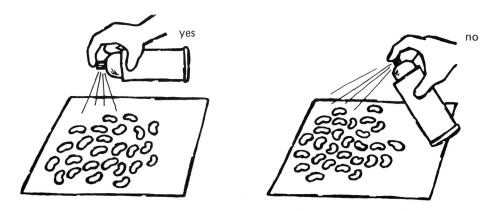

When the yellow paint is thoroughly dry, turn the beans over and spray paint the other side orange. Again, be especially careful to hold the can directly over the beans you are painting. When both sides are thoroughly dry, glue a yellow tail to the yellow side of the fish, and an orange tail to the orange side.

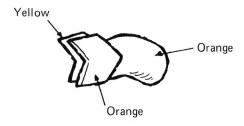

Make an eye and a mouth on each side.

Pour the finished yellow and orange fish into the separated area of the storage box.

NESTS

The child sets out various quantities or creates problems by placing eggs of two different colors in the birds' nests.

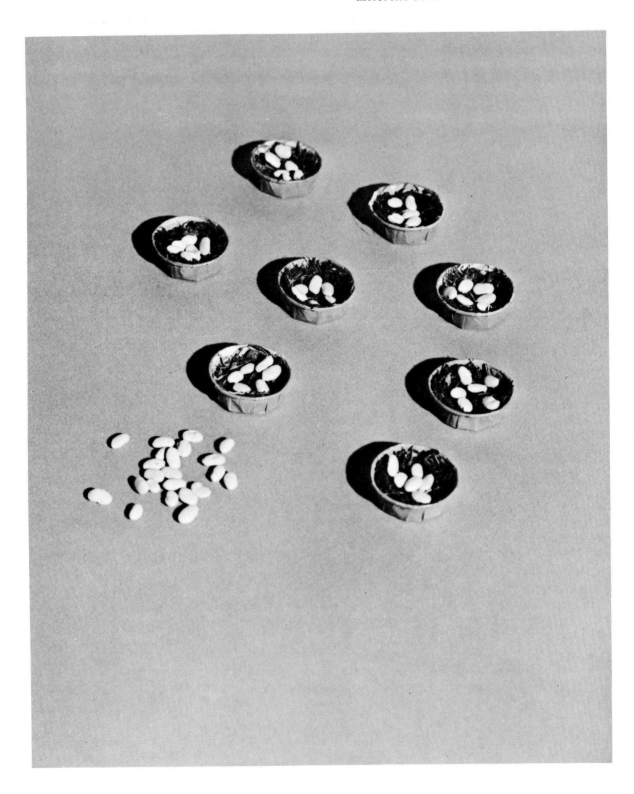

Materials

Storage Container

Storage box (approximately 9″ × 10″ × 1½″)

Separator strip of heavy cardboard

Counting Areas

Eight portion cups from a restaurant or janitorial supply outlet (or the bottoms cut out of eight paper cups)

Newspaper

Quick-drying brown spray paint

White glue

1/4 cup potting soil

One cup of grass clippings from mowing your lawn or cut with scissors at the park

Scissors

Plastic mixing bowl and spoon

Counters

1/4 cup great northerners or navy beans

Two cans of quick-drying spray paint to make beans look like bird eggs—pale yellow and baby blue are suggested

Making Directions

Label the opposite ends of a storage box "Eggs and Nests."

Glue separator strip inside on the bottom of the storage box.

Cut the grass clippings into approximately 3/4″ pieces. Spread them on a cookie sheet and bake at 300° for twenty minutes. This dries all the moisture out, but does not change the color.

Spread out several thicknesses of old newspaper and place the eight portion cups in the center. Spray lightly with brown spray paint. Mix the dry grass clippings and potting soil together with about 1/3 cup of white glue in a plastic mixing bowl. Put a spoonful of the mixture in the bottom of each painted portion cup and press it to the bottom and sides with your fingers to make a nest.

When they are dry, place the eight bird nests in the storage box.

Paint half the "eggs" with one color by rolling the beans from side to side in the bottom of a box while you depress the spray paint nozzle. When dry, take them out, put in the other half of the beans, and paint them with the second color. Pour the eggs into the separated area of the storage box.

TREES

Activity

The child sets out various quantities or creates problems by placing lights of two different colors on the green pine trees.

Materials

Storage Container

Storage box (approximately 9″ × 10″ × 1½″)

Separator strip of heavy cardboard

Counting Areas

A piece of dark green felt 7½″ × 5½″

Pattern for cutting out trees (see page 148)

Scissors

Eight pieces of royal blue railroad board (approximately 5½″ × 8½″)

White glue

Counters

Two different-colored strands of plastic faceted beads, 2′ long

Making Directions

Label opposite ends of a storage box "Pine Trees and Lights."

Glue separator strip inside bottom of storage box.

Cut out eight dark green felt trees with the pattern from the appendix. (You may prefer to Xerox or trace the pattern onto the paper rather than cutting it out so you keep the appendix intact.)

Glue each felt tree to a piece of royal blue railroad board with white glue.

Place the eight pine tree gameboards in the storage box.

Cut the beads off the two strands so they are all loose and place them in the separated area of the storage box.

PINCUSHIONS

Activity

The child sets out various quantities or creates problems by placing the pins in the two sides of the pincushions.

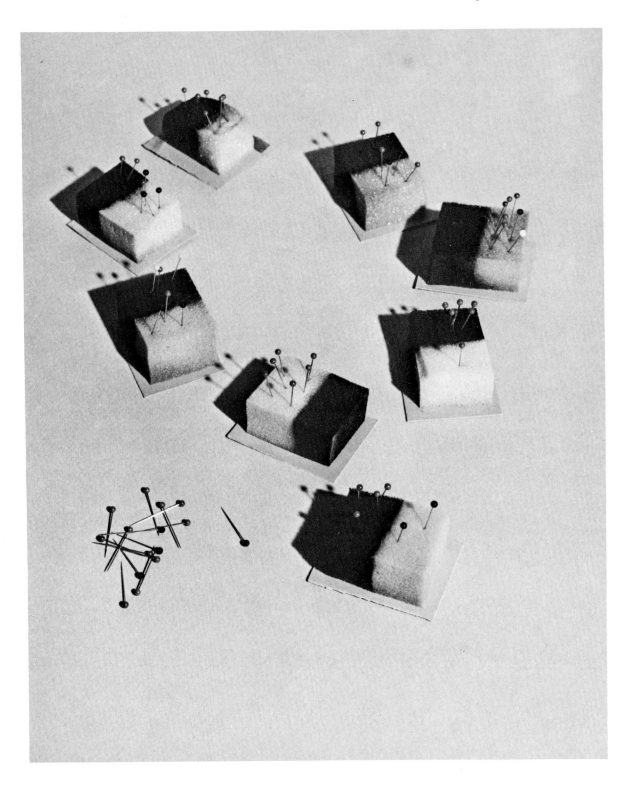

Materials

Storage container

Storage box (approximately 9″ × 10″ × 1½″)

Separator strip of heavy cardboard

Counting Areas

Eight pieces of foam rubber (approximately 1½″ × 2″ × 1″)

Eight pieces of railroad board (approximately 2″ × 2½″)

White glue

Newspapers

A scrap of tagboard 2½″ × 3½″

Two cans of quick-drying orange and brown spray paint

Counters

80 beaded pins

Making Directions

Label opposite ends of a storage box "Pins and Pincushions."

Glue separator strip inside bottom of storage box.

Spread out several thicknesses of old newspaper and put the eight pieces of foam in the center. Crease a 2½″ × 3½″ piece of tagboard so it fits snugly over the foam and exposes only half of it. Paint the exposed portion of each piece of foam with one color.

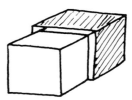

When it is dry, cover the painted portion with the tagboard and paint the other half with a second color. (It's not important to have the two halves exactly equal.) When dry, glue each piece of foam to a piece of 2″ × 2½″ railroad board with a generous amount of white glue.

Place the eight pincushions in the storage box.

Pour beaded pins into separated area of the storage box.

Note: This activity provides a good opportunity for young children to practice handling a potentially dangerous material safely and responsibly. During the teacher's initial introduction she or he should point out how to use pins safely and properly in this activity. The children should be asked directly, "Should pins be used to hurt people? Why not? Are they used to stick into pincushions?" Once this has been talked about openly there is rarely a problem and even if a problem should arise it provides an important opportunity to teach the child a needed lesson. Of course, it is left up to each classroom teacher to make the final judgement as to an individual student's ability to handle the material safely after having been properly instructed.

CHICKENS

Activity

The child sets out various quantities or creates problems by placing kernels of corn in the two feeding dishes which are pictured on each gameboard.

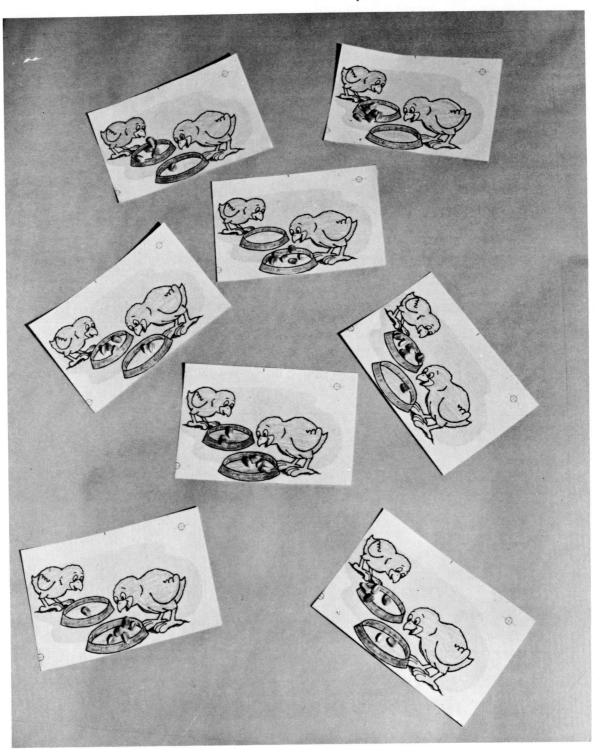

Materials

Making Directions

Storage Container

Storage box (approximately 9″ X 10″ X 1½″)

Separator strip of heavy cardboard

Label opposite ends of a storage box "Chickens and Corn."

Glue separator strip inside bottom of storage box.

Counting Areas

Eight chickens and corn gameboards (see page 143)

Crayons for coloring gameboards

Clear contact paper

Make a Thermofax master from the pattern in the appendix and run off eight chickens and corn gameboards on heavy tagboard. Color gameboards as desired with crayons. Cover gameboards with clear contact paper.

Place the chickens and corn gameboards in the storage box.

Counters

1/3 cup feed corn (from a feed store, not popcorn)

Pour corn into separated area of the storage box.

COOKIES

Activity

The child sets out various quantities or creates problems by placing chocolate and vanilla cookies together on the plates.

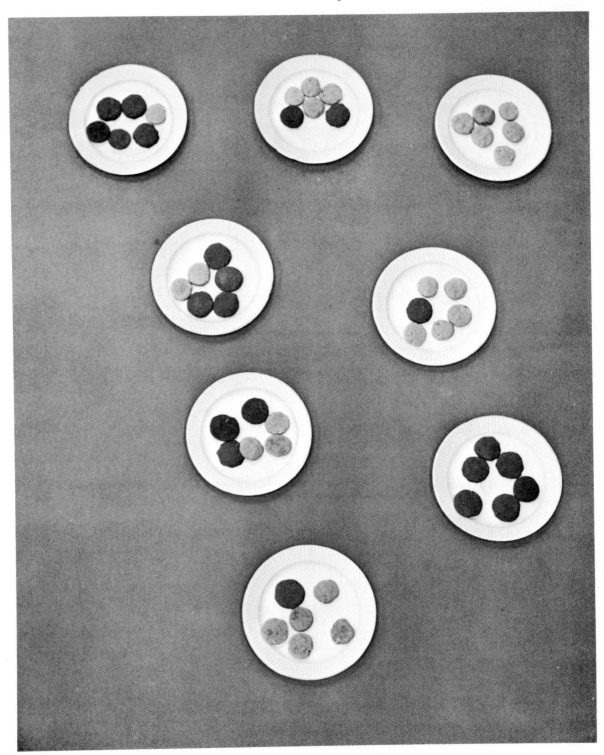

Materials

Storage Container

Storage box (approximately 9″ × 10″ × 1½″)

Separator strip of heavy cardboard

Counting Areas

Eight 6″ diameter paper plates

Counters

1 cup flour
½ cup salt

½ tsp. powdered yellow tempera paint

¼ cup water

Spoon, mixing bowl, cookie sheet

Make a second batch, substituting 2 tsp. powdered brown paint for the yellow

Making Directions

Label opposite ends of a storage box "Cookies."

Glue separator strip inside bottom of storage box.

Place the paper plates in the storage box.

Form the cookie dough into little balls. Press each ball of dough flat, making the cookies about the size of a nickel. Put cookies on a cookie sheet and bake at 250° for four hours. Turn once every hour.

Pour cookies into separated area of the storage box.

AIRPORTS

Activity

The child sets out various quantities or creates problems by placing airplanes on the divided runways.

Materials

Storage Container

Storage box (approximately 9" X 10" X 1½")

Separator strip of heavy cardboard

Counting Areas

Eight airport runway gameboards (see page 144)

Crayons for coloring gameboards

Clear contact paper

Counters

10 packages of Stim-u-dents (obtained from drug stores and dentists; these are interdental stimulators used to clean between the teeth)

White glue

Waxed paper

Silver spray paint

Newspaper

Making Directions

Label opposite ends of a storage box "Airports."

Glue separator strip inside bottom of storage box.

Make thermofax master using the pattern in the appendix and run off eight airport runway gameboards on heavy tagboard.

Color gameboards as desired with crayons.

Cover gameboards with clear contact paper.

Place the airport gameboards in the storage box.

Open the package of "Stim-u-dents" and break them apart into groups of three.

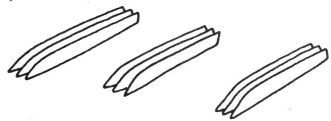

Each of these groups will make one airplane. Break one stick away from each of the other two. Line up the double sticks on a piece of waxed paper with the flat side down and the curved side up. Squeeze out a line of white glue, generously filling each trough. Don't skimp on the glue—it dries clear.

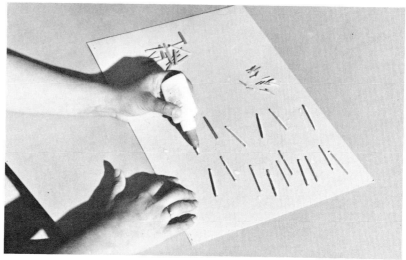

At this point, lay each single Stim-u-dent stick onto this model one at a time and mark the cut line with a pencil. (You can "eyeball" this if you prefer.)

Hold the stick between your fingernails at the point and break the point off.

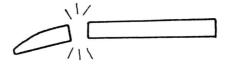

Stick this pointed, broken-off piece (thin side down) into the glue.

When the bodies and tails of the planes are dry, line up all the sticks from which you have broken the tail pieces. These sticks will form the wings on the bottom of each plane's body.

Put a generous dollop of glue in the center of each wing. Then press the body of a plane into the glue to dry. When the airplanes are thoroughly dry they can be painted with silver spray paint.

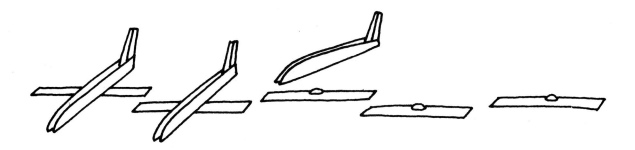

Put the airplanes in the storage box on top of the gameboards.

WATERMELON

Activity

The child sets out various quantities or creates problems by placing seeds on the slices of watermelon.

WORKJOBS II Correspondence Course

Teachers who wish to use the twenty WORKJOBS II activities in their classrooms can either collect the materials on their own using the composite list on pages 122–124, or mail in the attached postage paid cards to receive information for the Center for Innovation in Education's WORKJOBS II correspondence course.

The correspondence course, which was a dream of Mary's from the time of the publication of the first WORKJOBS book, is provided entirely through the mail as a service to teachers.

The course includes:
1. The WORKJOBS II Correspondence Course booklet.
2. All the materials listed and pictured in the appendix, enabling the teacher to make all 20 activities at once.
3. The option of earning two semester units of graduate credit.

The teacher can actually complete all twenty activities in two days by following the instructions and organizational procedure outlined in the correspondence booklet with all the needed materials at hand.

NOTE: It is assumed that a teacher taking the WORKJOBS II Correspondence Course has access to a copy of the book WORKJOBS II.

For information on the Center for Innovation in Education's WORKJOBS II Correspondence Course

MAIL THIS CARD or your name and address to:

WORKJOBS II
Center for Innovation In Education
19225 Vineyard Lane
Saratoga, CA 95070

Please send me information on the Center for Innovation in Education's WORKJOBS II Correspondence Course.

Name _____

Address _____

City _____ State _____ Zip _____

Mail this card or a letter listing the titles of the following books on which you would like information:

By Mary Baratta-Lorton for Kindergarten, 1st and 2nd grades:
WORKJOBS
WORKJOBS FOR PARENTS
WORKJOBS II
MATHEMATICS *THEIR* WAY

By Bob Baratta-Lorton for 3rd–6th grades:
MATHEMATICS . . . A WAY OF THINKING

Write: Addison-Wesley Publishing Co.
Innovative Division
2725 Sand Hill Road
Menlo Park, CA 94025

☐ Please send a brochure and ordering information for each of the books I have checked.

☐ Please ship immediately each of the books I have checked and bill me.

☐ WORKJOBS by Mary Baratta-Lorton
☐ WORKJOBS FOR PARENTS by Mary Baratta-Lorton
☐ WORKJOBS I I by Mary Baratta-Lorton
☐ MATHEMATICS *THEIR* WAY by Mary Baratta-Lorton
☐ MATHEMATICS. . . A WAY OF THINKING by Bob Baratta-Lorton
☐ Addison-Wesley Manipulatives to accompany MATHEMATICS *THEIR* WAY

Name _____

Address _____

City _____ State _____ Zip _____

WORKJOBS—An early childhood teacher resource book featuring 104 language arts and mathematics readiness activities which use everyday materials. Each activity photo-illustrated and described in detail. The most asked-for classic for early childhood education.

WORKJOBS. . .FOR PARENTS—Fifty-two manipulative tasks made from inexpensive materials for parents to use with young children. Adapted from the popular WORKJOBS (see above). Features a discussion of how to best use activity-centered learning in the home.

MATHEMATICS *THEIR* **WAY**—An activity-centered mathematics curriculum including more than 200 experiences which use familiar materials Includes sample teaching strategies and suggested dialog, 600 illustrative photos, answers to typical teachers' questions, an easy-to-manage assessment system, and a pad of black line masters for student worksheets.

MATHEMATICS . . . A WAY OF THINKING—A non-reading mathematics curriculum for grades 3–6, emphasizing successful learning experiences for students having trouble with math. Continues and expands the activity-centered approach of MATHEMATICS *THEIR* WAY, and leads to mathematics concepts beyond arithmetic while developing and clarifying basic skills. Includes suggested teaching dialog, step-by-step illustrations, and black line masters for student worksheets.

 **WORKJOBS**

 **MATHEMATICS** *THEIR* **WAY**

 **MATHEMATICS . . . A WAY OF THINKING**

MAIL THIS CARD or write for information about:

The Center for Innovation in Education's WORKJOBS II Correspondence Course

WORKJOBS II
Center for Innovation in Education
19225 Vineyard Lane
Saratoga, CA 95070

MAIL THIS CARD or write for ordering information on the following books by Mary and Bob Baratta-Lorton:
    WORKJOBS
    WORKJOBS FOR PARENTS
    WORKJOBS II
    MATHEMATICS *THEIR* WAY
    MATHEMATICS . . . A WAY OF THINKING

Addison-Wesley Publishing Company
Innovative Division
2725 Sand Hill Road
Menlo Park, CA 94025

Materials

Storage Container

Storage box (approximately 9″ × 10″ × 1½″)

Separator strip of heavy cardboard

Counting Areas

Watermelon slice pattern (see page 148)

Eight pieces of yellow railroad board (5½″ × 8½″)

Eight pieces of red felt (4″ × 6″)

One piece of green felt (12″ × 3″)

One piece of white felt (1½″ × 12″)

Scissors

White glue

Making Directions

Label opposite ends of a storage box "Watermelon."

Glue separator strip inside bottom of storage box.

Fold the piece of green felt in half and then in half again.

Place one of the folded edges against this model. Mark the cut lines on the felt with a pen or pencil.

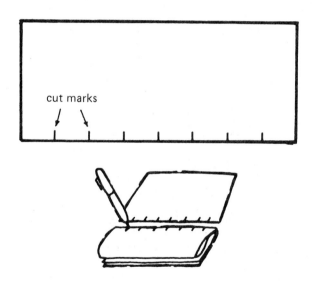

Mark the other folded edge in the same way.

Now cut the felt through the markings from folded edge to folded edge. This gives you eight long thin pieces. You want these pieces a bit uneven; just eyeball each cut and snip!

Repeat the whole procedure for the white piece of felt. This piece is narrower than the green one, so you'll end up with eight very skinny pieces. Again, don't try to make these cuts especially straight. You want them a bit uneven so the finished watermelon slices look more varied and natural.

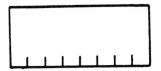

Trace the pattern for the watermelon slice from the appendix and use it to cut out eight pieces from the red felt. Glue each slice down on yellow railroad board. Put a line of glue around the curved edge of the red felt.

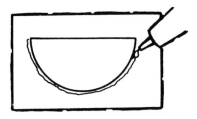

Press a white felt strip into the line of glue, forming it around the curved edge. Put another line of glue next to the white felt and press a green felt strip into this glue. You will find that the straight pieces curve quite easily.

Place the watermelon gameboard in the storage box.

Counters

1/4 cup baby lima beans

Quick-drying black
spray paint

Newspapers

Dump the baby lima beans into a piece of spread out newspaper, making sure they are close together but not actually touching. Spray this side black by holding the can of paint directly perpendicular to the beans. This prevents the mist from reaching the other side. Again, make sure the newspaper extends 2' beyond the beans to catch the overspray.

Pour watermelon seeds into separated area of the storage box.

HALLOWEEN

Activity

The child sets out various quantities or creates problems by placing the ghosts and pumpkins onto the haunted house on each gameboard.

Materials

Storage Container

Storage box (approximately 9″ X 10″ X 1½″)

Separator strip of heavy cardboard

Counting Areas

Eight pieces of buff-colored railroad board

Eight pieces of black felt 6″ X 8″

Haunted house pattern (see page 147)

White glue

Counters

3/4 cup large lima beans

Newspaper

Orange spray paint

Black fine line permanent marking pen, such as Sharpie by Sanford

Making Directions

Label opposite ends of a storage box "Halloween."

Glue separator strip inside the bottom of the storage box.

Cut eight haunted houses from black felt using the pattern in the appendix.

Glue each house to a piece of buff-colored railroad board with white glue.

Place the eight haunted house gameboards in the storage box.

Spread out a piece of old newspaper and put roughly half of the large lima beans in the center (don't count; it doesn't have to be exact).

Spray both sides of the beans orange.

While the orange paint is drying, draw the eyes for the ghosts on both sides of the unpainted portion of the beans using a fine line permanent marker.

When the orange paint is thoroughly dry, draw in the jack-o-lantern faces on both sides of the orange beans.

Double check to be sure the pumpkins and ghosts have faces on both sides and then place them in the separated area of the storage box.

Special thanks to Donna Burk, a teacher in San Jose, California, who dreamed up the Halloween Workjob for her kindergarten class and was happy to let me share her idea with you.

SPAGHETTI

Activity

The child sets out various quantities or creates problems by placing spaghetti and meatballs together on the paper plates.

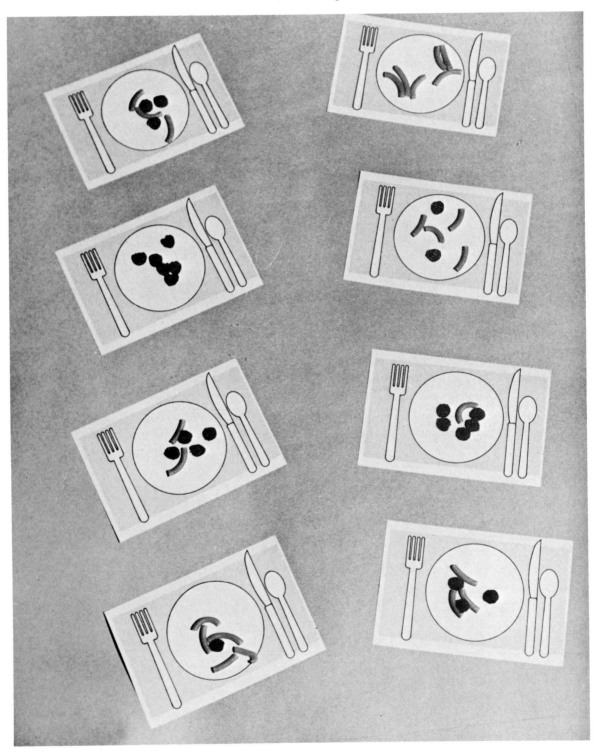

Materials

Making Directions

Storage Container

Storage box (approximately 9″ × 10″ × 1½″)

Separator strip of heavy cardboard

Label opposite ends of a storage box "Spaghetti and Meatballs."

Glue separator strip inside bottom of storage box.

Counting Areas

Eight spaghetti gameboards (see page 143)

Crayons for coloring gameboards

Clear contact paper

Scissors

Make a Thermofax master from the pattern in the appendix and run off eight gameboards on heavy tagboard. Color gameboards with crayons of desired color. Cover with clear contact paper.

Place "Spaghetti and Meatballs" gameboards in the storage box.

Counters

1/2 cup elbow macaroni

1 yard of red ball trim (½″ balls)

Scissors

Cut red "meatballs" from the ball trim and put them along with the macaroni into the separated area of the storage box.

MOUSETRAPS

Activity

The child sets out various quantities or creates problems by placing black-eared, black-tailed mice and pink-eared, pink-tailed mice.

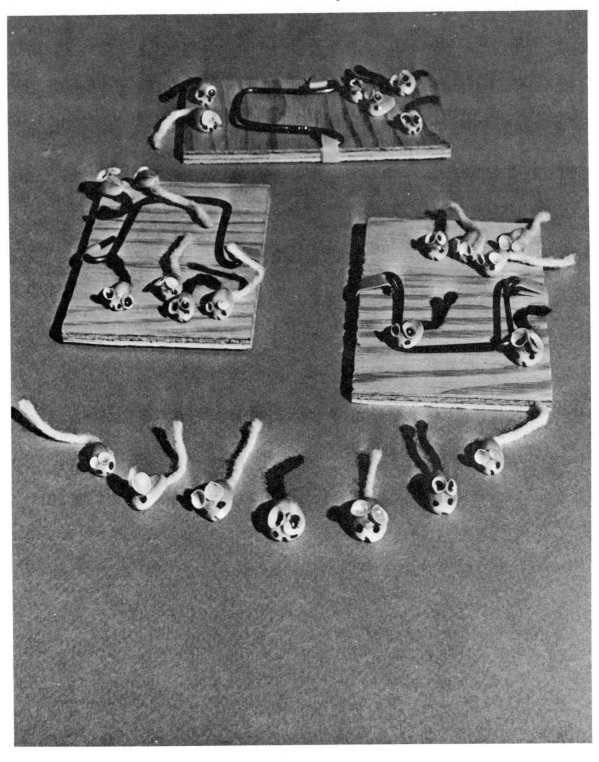

Materials

Storage Container

Storage box (approximately 9″ × 10″ × 1½″)

Separator strip of heavy cardboard

Counting Areas

Eight pieces of ¼″ plywood approximately 3″ × 5″

Eight heavy duty rubber bands (2 3/4″ × 3/8″)

Eight pieces of wire 8″ long cut from clothes-hangers with wire bolt cutters

Pliers

Making Directions

Label opposite ends of a storage box "Mousetraps."

Glue separator strip inside bottom of storage box.

Bend each wire with the pliers into a "mousetrap" wire shape according to the pattern in the appendix. Don't attempt to make them perfect or all alike; the more uneven they are the cuter they look.

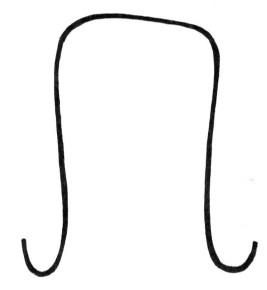

Slip one end of one heavy-duty rubber band over the end of the wire and pinch it shut with the pliers.

Put the wire on top of one piece of plywood and stretch the rubber band under the wood. Attach this free end to the wire and pinch that piece shut, securing the rubber band which in turn holds the wire in place.

Place the mousetraps in the storage box.

Counters

1/2 cup cowry and 1/8 cup rosecup sea shells

Model airplane glue

Black fine line marking pen with permanent ink

Red (or pink) yarn or rubber bands

Black yarn or rubber bands

Scissors

Line up all the cowry seashells and put a dollop of glue where each ear should go. Place the rosebud shell on the glue. Repeat to make all of the mice.

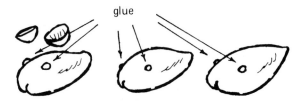

glue

When the ears are dry, divide the mice roughly in half—don't count, the exact number is not important. Cut enough 1″ pieces of pink yarn or rubber band for one group of mice and enough 1″ pieces of black yarn or rubber band for the other group. Put some glue on the bottom of each mouse and glue on their tails securely.

When the tails are dry, draw eyes on each mouse with the marking pen and color a black splotch on the ears of the mice with black tails. Be careful to put black splotches only on the ears of mice with black tails!

APPLES

Activity

The child sets out various quantities or creates problems by placing red and green apples in the buckets.

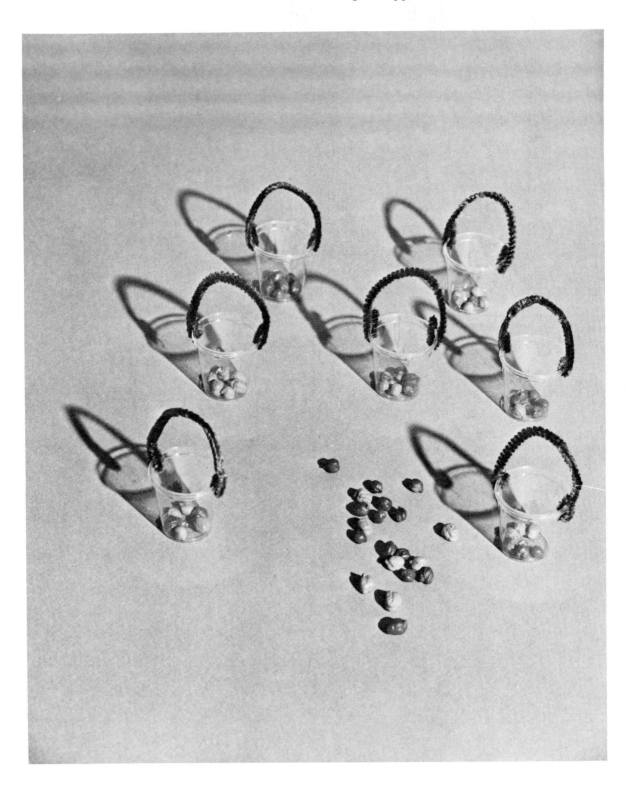

Materials	**Making Directions**

Storage Container

Storage box (approximately 9″ × 10″ × 1½″)

Separator strip of heavy cardboard

Label opposite ends of a storage box "Apples and Buckets."

Glue separator strip inside bottom of storage box.

Counting Areas

Eight plastic buckets (pharmacists and hospitals use them as medicine cups)

A large paper clip

Candle and matches

Eight 6″ pipe cleaners

Straighten out one end of a large paper clip.

Light a candle or put a large kitchen match in a lump of clay and light it. Hold the straight end of the paper clip in the flame for about 45 seconds and then push it quickly through both sides and then back out of the plastic bucket (just below the lip). This makes a hole through which you can thread the ends of a pipe cleaner to make the bucket's handle. Twist the end of each pipe cleaner around the handle above the lip so it can't pull through when the bucket is picked up.

Place the buckets in the storage box.

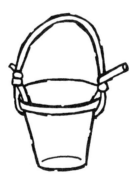

Counters

1/3 cup garbanzo beans

Two cans quick-drying spray paint (red and green)

Take one color of spray paint and paint the apples by rolling half of them from side to side in the bottom of a box while you depress the spray nozzle. Take them out of the box when they are dry and put in the other half. Paint them the other color.

Pour the apples into the separated area of the storage box.

LEAVES

The child sets out various quantities or creates problems by placing light and dark green leaves together on the tree which is pictured on the gameboards.

Materials

Storage Container

Storage box (approximately 9″ × 10″ × 1½″)

Separator strip of heavy cardboard

Counting areas

Eight leaves gameboards (see page 144)

Crayons for coloring gameboards

Clear contact paper

Counters

Two pieces of felt 9″ × 12″ (light green and dark green)

Scissors

Making Directions

Label opposite ends of a storage box "Leaves and Trees."

Glue separator strip inside bottom of storage box.

Make a Thermofax master from the pattern in the appendix and run off eight "Leaves" gameboards on heavy tagboard. Color gameboards with crayon. Cover with clear contact paper.

Trace this leaf pattern and use it as a guide to cut as many dark and light green leaves as possible from the felt. (It's fine to have a different amount of each color.)

Put the green leaves in the separated area of the storage box.

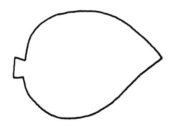

STRAWBERRIES

Activity

The child sets out various quantities or creates problems by placing red and green strawberries on the strawberry patches.

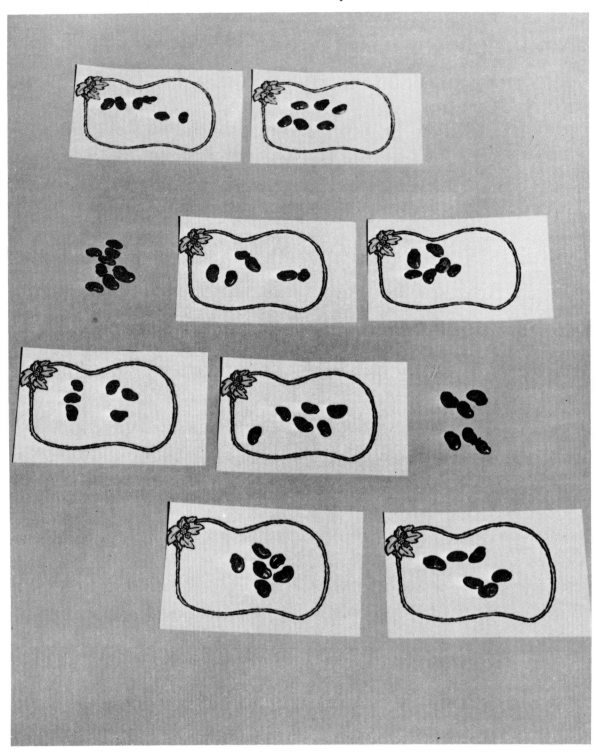

Materials

Making Directions

Storage Container

Storage box (approximately 9" X 10" X 1½")

Separator strip of heavy cardboard

Label opposite ends of a storage box "Strawberry Patch."

Glue separator strip inside bottom of storage box.

Counting Areas

Eight strawberry patch gameboards (see page 146)

Crayons

Clear contact paper

Make a Thermofax master from the pattern in the appendix and run off eight strawberry patch gameboards on heavy tagboard. Color gameboards with crayons of desired color. Cover with clear contact paper.

Place the strawberry patch gameboards in the storage box.

Counters

3/4 cup large lima beans

Two cans of quick-drying spray paint (red and green)

Felt scraps from cutting out green pine trees

Newspapers

White glue

Black fine line permanent marking pen

Spread out several thicknesses of old newspapers. Place the lima beans in the center very close together but not touching. Spray paint the beans red on this side. Hold the can directly over the beans so the mist is directed straight down rather than at an angle.

When the red paint is thoroughly dry, turn the beans over and paint the second side green. Again be careful to hold the can perpendicular to the beans.

Trace the pattern on this page and cut enough green felt strawberry tops so you have one for each lima bean. It is not necessary that these be done very carefully—they look good even if they're cut out very quickly without the pattern.

When both sides of the beans are thoroughly dry, glue a felt strawberry top onto each one with white glue and put "seeds" on each berry with a dot of black ink from the marking pen.

Pour strawberries into the separated area of the storage box.

FROGS AND TOADS

Activity

The child sets out various quantities or creates problems by placing frogs and toads together in the ponds.

Materials

Storage Container

Storage box (approximately 9″ × 10″ × 1½″)

Separator strip of heavy cardboard

Counting Areas

Eight pieces of brown railroad board (5½″ × 8½″)

Eight pieces of blue felt (4½″ × 6″)

Scissors

White glue

Making Directions

Label opposite ends of a storage box "Frogs and Toads."

Glue separator strip inside bottom of storage box.

Cut out an irregular pond shape from each piece of blue felt and glue it to the brown railroad board.

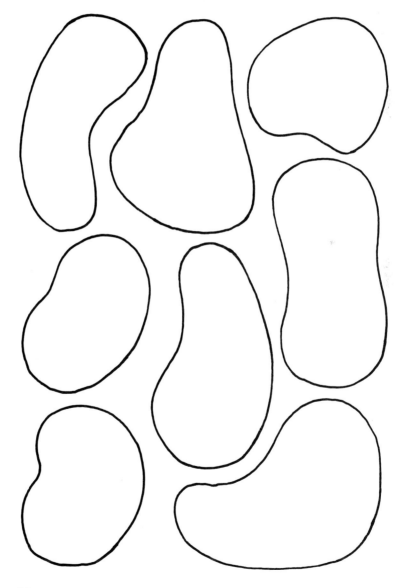

Place the pond gameboards in the storage box.

Counters

1¼ cups large lima beans

1/8 cup lentils

White glue

Two cans of quick-drying spray paint (brown and green)

Newspapers

Black fine line permanent marking pen

Make a line of large lima beans and put a big splotch of white glue on top of each. Don't skimp on the glue! (It dries completely clear.) Press a second lima bean into each splotch of glue.

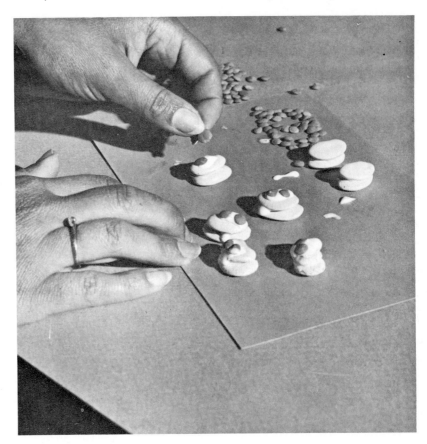

Put more glue on top and press two lentils into the glue to make the eyes.

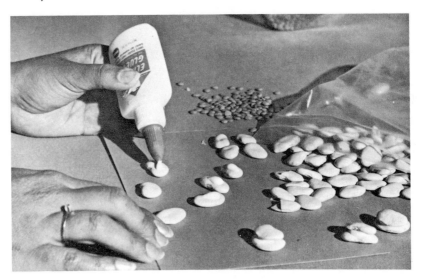

Make sure they're near the rounded edge of the limas, not in the center. *Do not* skimp on the glue! Use more than you think you need to! Some teachers even go back over the "eyeballs" when dry and cover them again with a blob of glue. It seeps down around the lentils and dries perfectly clear.

When throughly dry (twelve hours) spray paint half the lima beans brown and the other half green. (Don't count, just divide them roughly in half.)

Make an "eyeball" on the edge of each lentil and draw in a mouth.

Pour the frogs and toads into the separated area of the storage box.

BACON AND EGGS

Activity

The child sets out various quantities or creates problems by placing eggs and slices of bacon on the plates.

Materials

Storage Container

Storage box (approximately 9″ × 10″ × 1½″)

Separator strip of heavy cardboard

Counting Areas

Eight colored paper plates (may be spray painted if necessary)

Counters

Bacon pattern (see page 83)

Egg template patterns (see page 149)

One piece of white felt (7½″ × 12″)

One piece of yellow felt (1½″ × 12″)

One piece of brown felt (3″ × 12″)

White glue

Scissors

Making Directions

Label opposite ends of a storage box "Bacon and Eggs."

Glue separator strip inside bottom of storage box.

Place the paper plates in storage box.

Cut out egg yolks from yellow felt approximately the size shown on this page.

Trace a copy of the "egg templates" from the appendix onto plain paper. Place the template on top of the felt and poke through each dot with a pencil, marking the felt below.

Glue a felt egg yolk over each dot with white glue.

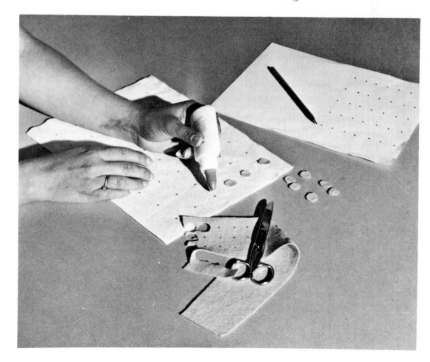

When the glue is dry, cut around each yolk, making irregular egg shapes.

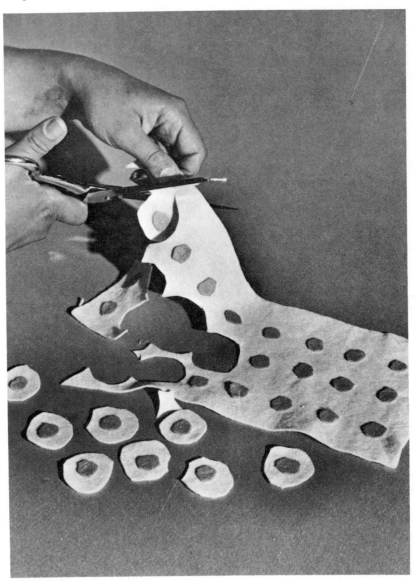

Take the piece of brown felt and cut it half, making two 1½″ × 12″ pieces.

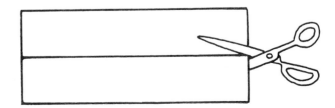

Cut each piece of 1½″ × 12″ brown felt apart, making wavy lines
to simulate bacon slices.

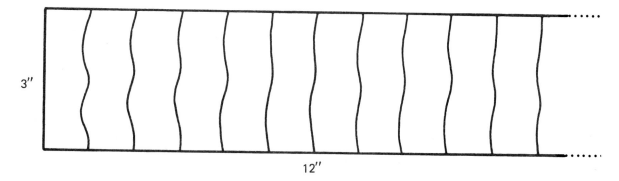

3″

12″

SNAPSHOTS

Activity

The child sets out various quantities or creates problems by positioning men's and women's faces for the photographer pictured on the gameboard.

Materials

Storage Container

Storage box (approximately 9″ × 10″ × 1½″)

Separator strip of heavy cardboard

Counting Areas

Eight snapshots gameboards (see page 146)

Crayons

Clear contact paper

Counters

1 cup fava beans (or 3/4 cup lima beans sprayed light brown to simulate flesh tones)

Brown or black felt scraps

White glue

Scissors

Black fine line permanent marking pen

Making Directions

Label opposite ends of a storage box "Snapshots."

Glue separator strip inside bottom of storage box.

Make a Thermofax master from the pattern in the appendix and run off eight gameboards on heavy tagboard. Color gameboards as desired, with crayons. Cover with clear contact paper.

Place gameboards in the storage box.

Cut 1/2″ × 1″ rectangles from black or brown felt scraps for hair.

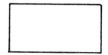

Cut the corners off each felt rectangle.

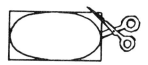

Glue the felt to the top of each bean folding it to bring the hair down on both sides of the bean.

Cut a 1/8″ × 3/4″ rectangle of felt for each man's mustache. Glue in position on only one side of each bean.

When the glue is dry, draw in eyes and mouths.

Put faces into the separated area of the storage box.

BIRTHDAY CAKES

Activity

The child sets out various quantities or creates problems by placing candles of two colors on the birthday cake gameboards.

Materials

Making Directions

Storage Container

Storage box (approximately 9" X 10" X 1½")

Separator strip of heavy cardboard

Label opposite ends of a storage box "Birthday Cakes."

Glue separator strip into bottom of storage box.

Counting Areas

Frosting pattern (see page 147)

Eight birthday cake gameboards (see page 145)

Crayons for coloring gameboards

Eight (3" X 5") pieces of pale yellow felt

Scissors

White glue

Clear contact paper

X-Acto knife or single-edged razor blade

Make a Thermofax master from the pattern in the appendix and run off eight gameboards on heavy tagboard. Color gameboards as desired, with crayons. Cover with clear contact paper.

Cut through the contact paper around the top of each cake with an X-Acto knife or single-edged razor blade, being careful not to cut into the tagboard.

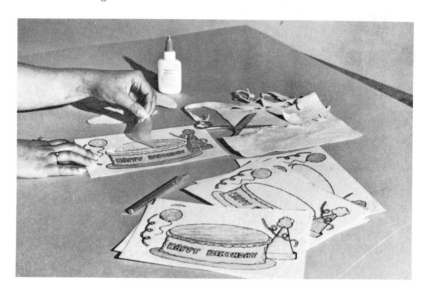

Peel the contact paper off the top of each cake so the tagboard is exposed. Using the frosting pattern from the appendix, cut out eight identical pieces of yellow felt and glue them onto the exposed tagboard portion of each gameboard with white glue.

Counters

Two boxes (36 candles in each) in two different colors

Pour candles into the separated area of the storage box.

RIVER ROCKS

Activity

The child sets out various quantities or creates problems by placing the river rocks in the divided stream which is pictured on the gameboards.

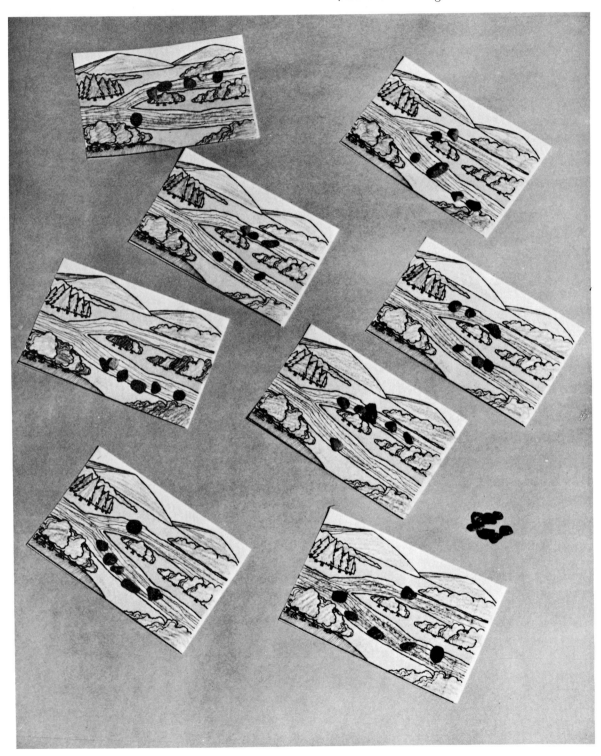

Materials

Storage Container

Storage box (approximately 9″ × 10″ × 1½″)

Separator strip of heavy cardboard

Counting Areas

Eight river rock gameboards (see page 145)

Crayons for coloring gameboards

Clear contact paper

Counters

1/2 cup of river rocks

Making Directions

Label opposite ends of a storage box "River Rocks."

Glue separator strip inside bottom of storage box.

Make a Thermofax master from the pattern in the appendix and run off eight "River Rocks" gameboards on heavy tagboard. Color gameboards as desired with crayons. Cover with clear contact paper.

Place the river rock gameboards in the storage box.

Pour river rocks into separated area of the storage box.

SANDY BEACHES

Activity

The child sets out various quantities or creates problems by placing shells in the ocean and on the sandy beach nearby.

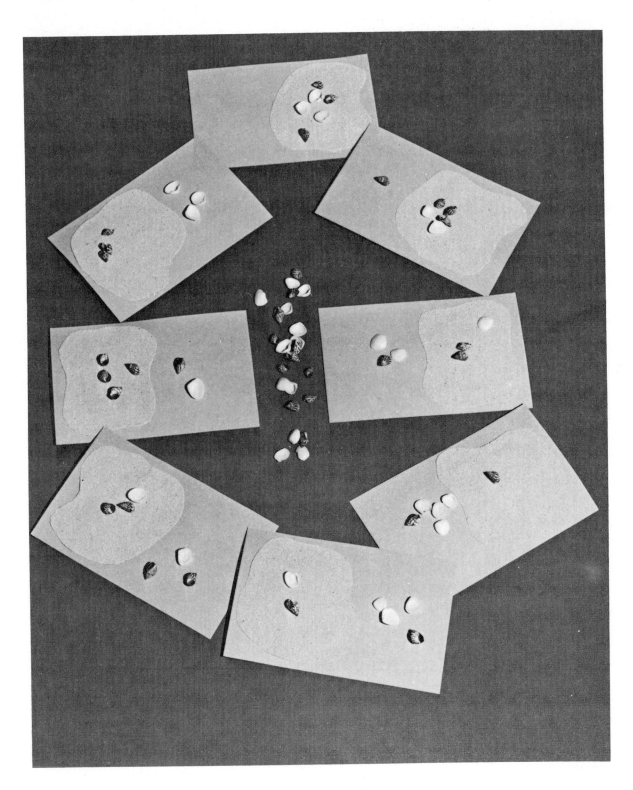

Materials

Storage Container

Storage box (approximately 9″ × 10″ × 1½″)

Separator strip of heavy cardboard

Counting Areas

Eight pieces of blue railroad board (5½″ × 8½″)

Eight 4″ × 4″ pieces of sand paper

Old pair of scissors

White glue

Counters

2/3 cup of small sea shells

Making Directions

Label opposite ends of a storage box "Sandy Beaches."

Glue separator strip inside bottom of storage box.

Cut out each shape with old scissors and glue them to one end of each piece of blue railroad board, leaving the other end as the "ocean" area.

Place the sandy beach gameboards in the storage box.

Pour shells into the separated area of the storage box.

PART IV

Presenting the Activities

Introducing the Activities to the Class

Once the twenty Workjobs activities are assembled you will be ready to begin using them in your classroom. Open half the boxes one day and show them to the children. As you open each box, ask the children to tell you what the two parts (the counters and the counting areas) are, for example: watermelon seeds and watermelon slices, tiny eggs and birds nests, mice and mousetraps, etc. The language development that results will give the children the appropriate words to use when talking with their friends as they work on their activities. The goal of this first day's lesson is for the children to become familiar with the activities and to learn how to use them correctly. Talk about being careful with the materials so as not to bend the gameboards or drop or step on the boxes, and to insure all the counters are back in the box at the conclusion of the activities. It is helpful to role play putting the individual boxes back onto the storage shelf.

When these things have been discussed, group the children into ten groups of three (if you have more than thirty children in your class, make some groups of four). You may want to demonstrate what you want each group to do before grouping the children. Give each group one box. Ask them to open their boxes, put out the eight gameboards and work together to put five counters on each gameboard. When the class has done this, ask the children to walk around the classroom—very carefully to avoid stepping on any materials—to look at all the different activities. When they have finished, have the class sit down again and take turns sharing with each other what they noticed.

A nice technique to encourage the children to listen to one another is to either write down each child's comments on a separate 9″ × 12″ piece of paper or to tape record them. At the end, shuffle the pages and then hold them up one at a time. As you read the comment ask the class to tell you who said it. Let the children keep their own comments to take home. If a tape was made the children listen to the comment and identify the child who spoke.

"I know why some strawberries were green! They're not ripe yet."

"There were ghosts and pumpkins in the haunted house!"

"Chickens eat corn—my mama feeds our big chickens that same kind of corn!"

"There are eight mouse traps and eight watermelons and eight of all of um!"

"Did you see those little eggs in the bird nests? We have a nest in the tree by my house and there are some baby birds in it."

When the children are finished talking, have them clean up. Call one child from each group (one at a time) to put the box back on the storage shelf. The class should watch while the teacher reminds the class to notice how carefully the box is carried and put away so the label is visible.

The next day you can open the last ten boxes and repeat the lesson from the day before.

On the third day open all twenty boxes and quickly review the words describing the counters and the counting areas.

Now the children are ready to begin.

For a few days the children can work in pairs with a box between them. They each take four counting areas and put some counters down. Then they tell their partner about their groups:

"I have three orange fish and two yellow ones and one orange one here, and way over there I have two orange and two yellow ones. . . ."

"Three pumpkins were in the haunted house and two ghosts scared the three pumpkins."

"There are five ghosts and two pumpkins in this house . . . over here are three, four . . . four ghosts and. . . ."

During this time, walk around the classroom encouraging the children to discuss their groups with their partner and reinforcing the correct way to handle and return the materials. The children should work for ten to fifteen minutes each day, selecting a second or third activity if there is time. The atmosphere should be relaxed and not rushed, keeping the focus on cooperation and conversation. During these few days the teacher should find a time during some other periods of the day when the children's skills with numbers can be assessed individually. Once the teacher has gathered this information, the children's work with the activities can be individualized and they can work on the skills which are appropriate to their own developmental level.

Assessing the Child's Concept of Number

Set up an area like this on a low table.

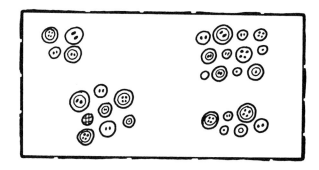

Ask the following question of each child in class one at a time.

"Count one of these piles of buttons, please."

By not specifying which pile to count, you will learn something in addition to the child's level of skill in counting. A child who begins with the group of twelve and counts it correctly saves you the time of finding this high level. A child who starts with the pile of twelve but counts it incorrectly gives you a clue as to how far they probably can count (the number at which they first get mixed up) as well as revealing that they may not recognize a task that is too difficult. As each child counts, watch his or her finger carefully, don't just listen. You're looking for information on the child's skill both with the sequence of number names and with 1:1 correspondence. (Resist the urge to ask anyone else to do this assessment for you, for from it you will gain many insights into the children which are lost to you forever when someone else assesses.)

POSSIBLE ASSESSMENT RESULTS

Kelly: "One, two, two, two, two, two."

1. Counting even the group of four objects is difficult. Kelly needs help learning the order of number names and developing 1:1 correspondence. She should start with the activities outlined in Part II (pages 22–23) as she is not yet ready for any of the activities in this Part.

James: "One, Two, Three, Four."
Teacher: "Will you choose another pile to count, please?"

James: "One, two, three, four, five, six, ten, elevendy."

2. Counting four objects is easy for James, but he has difficulty using the sequence of number names when counting eight objects. James should begin making groups of six objects with the WORKJOBS II materials. (Starting with the level of his success—counting to six.)

Melanie: "One, two, three, four."
Teacher: "Will you choose another pile to count, please?"

Melanie: "One, two, three, four, five six, seven, eight, nine, ten, eleven."

3. Counting the group of four objects is easy, but using a 1:1 correspondence when counting eight objects is difficult. Melanie knows the order of the number names but needs help with 1:1 correspondence. She should make groups of five with the WORKJOBS II activities. Melanie seemed to have 1:1 correspondence with four objects, and now needs to practice with five.

Bobby: "One, two, three, four."

Teacher: "Will you choose another pile to count, please?"

Bobby: "One, two, three, four, five, six, seven, eight."

Teacher: "Will you choose another pile to count, please?"

Bobby: (Counts correctly to twelve.)

4. Counting groups of four, eight, or twelve is easy.

Bobby clearly knows the order of number names and has the skill of 1:1 correspondence firmly established. He is ready for the Connecting Level assessment. (See page 105.)

Compiling an Assessment Record

Record each child's name under the number that identifies the level at which he or she needs help in learning the order of number names.

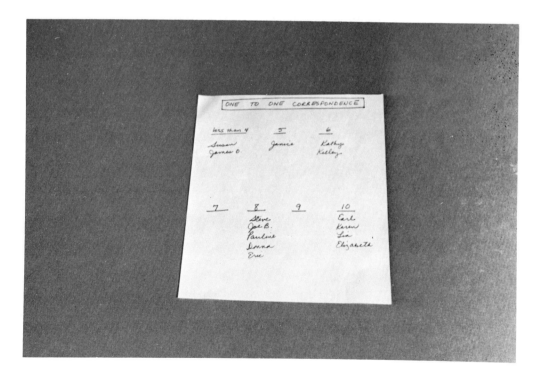

This list indicates the number of objects each child should count onto each gameboard regardless of the particular Workjob they choose. The children who can successfully count to ten are ready for the Connecting Level assessment on page 105.

The children who can only count to four need to develop the prerequisite skills described on pages 22–23 before they begin using the Workjobs.

A separate list can be made of the children who would benefit from two to three minutes of oral counting practice in a large group several time a day.*

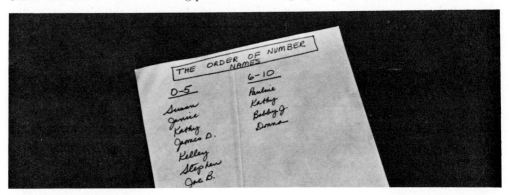

The class should begin counting to five and after several days or a week of success should count to six . . . gradually adding one new number in sequence. The children needing this practice benefit greatly from group modeling.

Using WORKJOBS II at the Concept Level

SKILLS DEVELOPED AT THE CONCEPT LEVEL

Children exploring number at the concept level with the WORKJOBS II materials develop skill in 1:1 correspondence by having many opportunities to create small groups of four to ten objects. The child builds many groups, each of identical quantity, so she or he may have sufficient practice at an appropriate level of difficulty. In addition to developing skill with 1:1 correspondence, the child discovers the quantitative relationships that exist within and between the numbers from 1–9.

WHAT IS THE CONCEPT LEVEL?

Exploration of number at the Concept Level is an opportunity for the children to discover and think about quantitative relationships in whatever way occurs naturally in their own minds, without any imposed structure from symbols or adult logic. *No written symbols are used* at this stage of development because written notation will actually cut the child off from his or her unique thinking process. (A symbol confines the attention to a specific numeral view of the material which narrows and limits the child's thinking.)

It is important to understand that children benefit from exploring the small numbers from 4–10 in far greater depth than they ordinarily have the opportunity to do. Within a number like *five* are many manageable relationships which a

---

*If there are even three or four children in your classroom who need oral counting practice, the whole class should work on counting activities for short periods several times each day. (See pages 92–100 in MATHEMATICS *THEIR* WAY.)

young child's mind can easily grasp. Five contains such number relationships as: four and one, one is three less than four, four is three more than one, four contains one less than five, three is two less than five, two and three combine to make five, four has two twos in it, etc. Every child intuits such relationships if they are allowed the unhurried time they need for exploring number.

It is difficult for young children to make comparisons spontaneously with larger quantities unless they have previously discovered and intuited the relationships within smaller ones. This is why it is so important to insure an atmosphere of acceptance and appreciation of the smaller quantities. The attitude expressed by, "Wow! Now you can count to eight!" hinders the appreciation of the special wonder of four or five in the mad dash for the all-worshiped ten!

The children should be allowed to stay at the Concept Level for as long as they continue to enjoy and be absorbed in the process of counting out groups of objects. Only when the child counts out ten objects with great ease and confidence, and seems a little bored, is that child ready for the next level. Each child clearly signals readiness through this combination of confidence and slight boredom. The teacher who waits and watches will in time increase his or her receptivity to these signals.

Experiences at the Concept Level provide each child with the basic foundation for all later levels and remain, of all subsequent levels, the most important for the child's conceptual development. The teacher and child should savor this stage for if a child is pressured to move ahead too quickly, the unique value offered by this level will be lost forever. We should wait for the child to push us, rather than us pushing the child.

HOW THE CHILD USES THE WORKJOBS AT THE CONCEPT LEVEL

Each child using WORKJOBS II at the Concept Level should explore at the level which is appropriate for him or her according to the assessment.

A child having difficulty counting to six is asked to count out sets of six on each gameboard.

The child will do this many different times on different days.

A child having difficulty counting to four is asked to count out sets of four onto each gameboard many different times.

A child who counts with ease and confidence to ten may be asked to count out sets of ten objects onto each gameboard and should be given the Connecting Level assessment.

By placing the same number of objects on *each* gameboard the child has many repeated opportunities to practice counting this quantity.

By working at their appropriate level the children do not spend time counting groups that are too easy or groups that are too difficult, but rather, concentrate all their time in practicing counting the quantity they need to practice counting. In this way, 1:1 correspondence is developed efficiently and effectively.

Each level can be thought of as a kind of assessment in itself. If a child is told to work at *five* but makes mistakes (e.g., placing four watermelon seeds on some slices, five on most others, and even six on a few), the teacher should *not* correct it on the spot. It is more effective for the teacher to make a note to ask the child the next day to put four objects, rather than five, on each board (backing up to the success level). When the child has four on each board she or he is asked to add one more object to each board and then to count each group of five with a friend. The time and energy spent reteaching a child *at an inappropriate level* (evidenced by the child making mistakes) does not produce as much gain as when you back up to a more appropriate level and let the child teach himself or herself. The next day, the child should be ready to try counting out five from the start. The child should count five objects, using new materials (airplanes, one day, perhaps, and spaghetti and meatballs the next), but repeating the activity of counting to five for many days in a row. When the teacher feels this work is too easy and the child seems a bit bored the child should be ready to try counting to six.

Using WORKJOBS II at the Connecting Level

SKILLS DEVELOPED

Children exploring number at the Connecting Level with the WORKJOBS II materials develop skill in number-numeral association by building sets of objects with quantities from 1–9 according to the direction of a specific number card or equation card.

WHAT IS THE CONNECTING LEVEL?

At the Connecting Level, the Workjobs link the concepts developed during the earlier Concept Level work with traditional mathematical symbolization. This level is a bridge from the familiar world of concrete materials to the adult world of abstraction and symbolization. The child does no writing at this stage but, rather, uses cards with symbols printed on them.

The child will count out groups of objects in three different ways at this level:

1. matching a quantity to a given mathematical symbol (numbers 0–9);

2. exploring and experiencing the process of addition;

3. exploring and experiencing the process of subtraction.

Each way represents a slightly different type of thinking; all are important and none is much more difficult than another.

Matching a Quantity to a Given Mathematical Symbol

The child counts out the correct number of objects to match a given numeral.

The Process of Addition

The child puts out the correct number of objects to represent a given combination.

The Process of Subtraction

The child puts out the correct number of objects . . . and then removes a portion of that group to show the process of subtraction.

A child at this stage should never be asked, "How many are there altogether?" or "How many remain?" because the emphasis in this stage is on the *process* of the operations. Remainders and totals are a separate step which is appropriate later (at the Symbolic Level), not here.

ADDITIONAL MATERIALS NEEDED

In the appendix you will find the five masters you will need for preparing numeral cards (page 137–138) and the four levels of equation cards (easier addition, page 139), easier subtraction (using only numerals 0–5, page 140), harder addition (using numerals 0–9, page 141), and harder subtraction (using numerals 0–9, page 142). Make ten of each for each classroom.

Each card above should be run off on heavy tagboard, covered with contact paper and then cut apart. The teacher can visually identify the five different levels from one another by rubbing lightly over the face of each set with the side of a crayon (with the paper removed), coloring each of the five sets differently. If the teacher has access to colored tagboard in five colors this would, of course, produce the same results.

ASSESSING THE CHILD'S READINESS

A child who is ready for the Connecting Level can effortlessly and confidently count out ten objects onto each gameboard and seems ready for a new challenge. To place a child suitably at this level, make a dittoed copy of the Assessment sheet on page 152 for each child who is ready to be tested. Point to each number one at a time, circling it if the child names it quickly, correctly, and with confidence.

INTERPRETING AND INDIVIDUALIZING FROM THE ASSESSMENT INFORMATION

1. If the child knows no number, write the numbers one, two, three, four and five on the front of a library pocket that has the child's name on it, and give the child two or three numeral cards each.* (See pages 137–138.)

*Even though, technically, the child only needs eight cards to match with eight gameboards in each Workjob, it is helpful if they have several extra cards. This gives the child more free choice as well as preventing the inevitable problem that arises if a child drops a card or two on the floor and then finds she or he doesn't have enough to put with the gameboards.

After a few weeks reassess each child. Assuming they now know the numbers from 1–5, continue to keep one of each number they know in their library pockets, and add two or three numeral cards of each number from 6–9 as well.

When the child knows all the numbers from 0–9, he or she can begin using the equation cards. These do not have dots on them, so the child must know all the numbers before beginning. (See pages 139–142.)

2. If the child knows a few numbers but not all, write the numbers the child needs to learn on the front of his or her library pocket.

Let the child dig through the box of number cards to find three of each number listed on the front of the library pocket.

3. If the child knows all the numbers from 0–9, or all but one, allow the child to select some equation cards to work with.

HOW THE CHILD USES THE ACTIVITIES AT THE CONNECTING LEVEL

Each child needs a library pocket with his or her name on the front. This library pocket can be kept pinned to the bulletin board with a push pin (which young children easily pin and unpin) or they can be collected at the end of each period and stored in a cut-off, half gallon milk carton.

Children working at the Connecting Level can use the Workjobs activities in the ways discussed on the following pages.

Exploring with Numeral and Equation Cards

The child matches either a numeral card or equation card to each of the eight empty counting areas of a Workjob.

Numeral cards are used by the children who cannot yet name all ten numerals (0–9) quickly and confidently. The dots by each numeral enable the children to count to identify the symbol thereby teaching *themselves,* in time, to identify each symbol.

Equation cards are used by the children who can identify all the symbols from 0–9 quickly and confidently.

Then the child fills each counting area with the appropriate counters as directed by the symbol or equation.

At the equation card level the goal is to have the child work like the child pictured above, exploring both addition and subtraction within the same activity. However, to get to this point gracefully usually takes about two weeks. It is best when there are five or six children ready for equation cards at once so they can work together in pairs during this introductory period.

Introducing the Processes of Addition and Subtraction

The children need about ten addition cards and should use these for two or three days, building addition problems on the eight counting areas of many different activities. After several days of addition practice the addition cards should be replaced with subtraction cards which then are used by the child exclusively for three to six days.

Introductory Subtraction Lesson

When first beginning subtraction the children need an introductory lesson (or two) like the following: The teacher demonstrates once and then asks the group to explain the process step-by-step.

The teacher verbalizes and demonstrates the steps in subtraction.

The children retell the subtraction steps to direct the teacher's actions:

The teacher's verbalization and demonstration potentially puts the needed information (the two steps) into the child's mind. Retelling the steps gives the child an opportunity to demonstrate knowledge and understanding of the steps as well as to see the demonstration a second time.

The children should now work in pairs and complete one activity. After working in pairs for several days, the children should work independently for two or three days on subtraction.

When the teacher senses that the children clearly understand the process, they are ready to select six addition and six subtraction cards and put them in their library pocket. These children are now ready to explore both addition and subtraction within the same Workjob activity.

A Photographic Collage of the Connecting Level

Activities with Numeral Cards

Easier addition equations (using only the numerals from 0–5)

Easier subtraction equations (using only the numerals from 0–5)

Harder addition equations (using numerals from 0–9)

Harder subtraction equations (using numerals from 0–9)

Using WORKJOBS II at the Symbolic Level

SKILLS DEVELOPED

Children exploring number at the Symbolic Level with the WORKJOBS II materials develop skills in symbolizing their own mathematical experiences. At this level children concretely represent and then record the experience in three different ways:

1. Using one numeral to identify a set of objects.

2. Using two numerals and the appropriate sign to identify the process of addition and subtraction.

3. Recording the process and the resulting solutions for a variety of addition and subtraction equations (the focus is on the totals or remainders).

ASSESSING THE CHILD'S READINESS

When a child has worked for several weeks with the easier addition and subtraction equation cards, and then for several more weeks with the harder addition and subtraction equation cards and can correctly and effortlessly write the numbers from zero through nine (see page 23) the child is ready for the additional challenges provided at the Symbolic Level.

ADDITIONAL MATERIALS NEEDED

The teacher will need to prepare three additional materials:

1. Small pieces of paper, cut from 8½″ X 11″ newsprint as shown here

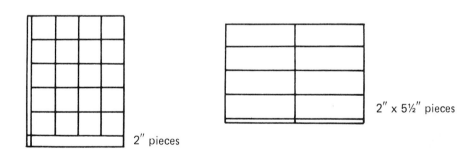

2″ pieces

2″ x 5½″ pieces

2. Tiny book covers

3. Tiny book tally charts

1. The teacher should cut 50–100 (8½″ × 11″) sheets of newsprint (or some other inexpensive paper). These can be stored in a box and should be placed where the children have easy access to them at all times.

2. Book covers: The children need access to a stapler and dittoed copies of the "tiny book covers" (masters are on pages 150 and 151). The cover has a place marked for stapling. This guides the child to fasten the book together with only two staples. (Teachers who have had their stapler repeatedly jammed or seen their children delightedly perseverate and staple their material completely closed using ten to one hundred staples will appreciate this simple, foolproof innovation.)

The teacher runs the tiny book covers off on regular ditto paper, cuts them apart and stores them in a plastic bag fixed to a bulletin board (for easy access by the children).

3. Tally charts: The teachers should make the following charts on butcher paper or tagboard as the children move into the Symbolic Level and begin making "tiny books." The children's names are added to the chart one at a time when they complete their first tiny book. Each time another book is completed the teacher puts a tally after the child's name, making a simple and informal record of the work that has gone home.

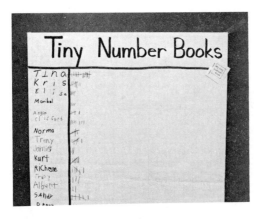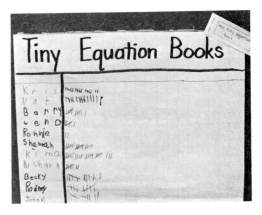

WHAT IS THE SYMBOLIC LEVEL?

The Symbolic Level provides many opportunities for children to make written records using traditional mathematical symbols.

Except for writing a single numeral to identify a set of objects, the Symbolic Level is not appropriate for kindergarten and should not be begun until first grade. Kindergarten teachers will want to offer activities to broaden the experiences of their advanced children rather than getting more abstract.* This is especially critical because once our advanced kindergarten children reach first grade they will be given only activities requiring progressively greater abstraction. If *we* don't broaden their understanding, who will?

There are three different steps at the Symbolic Level:

A. Making numeral cards and equation cards

B. Recording addition and subtraction equations with the totals and remainders

C. Making up problems

Step A: Making numeral cards

The children either: 1) write a single number on a piece of paper and then put out the appropriate number of objects on each counting area from one of the Workjobs; or 2) first set up their boards with counters and then record the descriptive number.

When the children finish they gather up their papers and put a "tiny *number* book" cover on the front, stapling it at the two designated places. (The teacher will want to demonstrate this to the children.) The book can now be tallied on the chart and sent home.

*Activities such as counting jars of objects and estimating and graphing (pages 310 and 319) in MATHEMATICS *THEIR* WAY done independently make good Concept Level alternatives.

Step A: Making equation cards

Make addition equation cards without totals. The child puts out any desired number of objects onto each counting area.

The child then records the resulting addition combinations on a small piece of paper. Totals are not yet recorded because the focus is only on recording the process of addition.

| 3 + 4 | 2 + 3 | 6 + 0 | 4 + 1 | 5 + 5 |

This activity can be repeated for subtraction as well.

Step B: Recording the answers to addition and subtraction equations

This step encourages the children to solve both addition and subtraction problems within the same lesson. The child puts an addition or subtraction equation card with each counting area and builds the appropriate concrete representation of each.

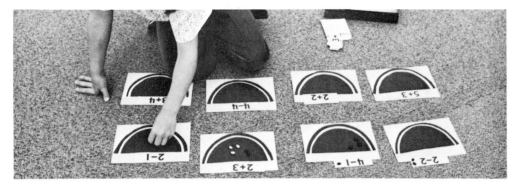

Now the child puts a blank piece of paper (2″ × 6″) with each counting area and records both the problem and the answer.

When the children finish they gather up their papers and put a "tiny *equation* book" cover on the front, stapling at the two designated places. (The teacher will want to demonstrate this to the children.) This book can be tallied on a chart and then can go home.

Step C: Making up problems

The child makes up his or her own problems on the counting areas (using any of the Workjobs) recording them either on 2″ × 6″ pieces of newsprint or on a dittoed sheet (see page 153 of the Appendix). The child should not be required to fill every space with equations.

At this stage it seems to work best if the child uses only one counting area which is cleared at the end of each problem and revised for the next. This provides maximum freedom to create large problems.

Using the Activities to Explore Place Value, Multiplication and Division

Children who are ready to explore the numbers above ten should first be exposed to the place value counting game and the activities described on pages 276–306 in MATHEMATICS *THEIR* WAY and in issue III of the MATHEMATICS *THEIR* WAY NEWSLETTER.* These activities give children the necessary and appropriate experiences to enable them to discover and to understand the structure of our base ten number system. Once the children have had these experiences, they will benefit from using WORKJOBS II activities to build large numbers and to explore multiplication or division.

*Available at cost, from the Center for Innovation in Education, 19225 Vineyard Lane, Saratoga, CA 95070.

"three tens and six"

"one ten and eight"

"two tens and five"

"seven tens and one"

EXPLORING MULTIPLICATION

The teacher makes a stack of cards like the ones shown above for the children to use to explore division. None should have remainders. The back of each card shows the total number of objects (the dividend) in groups of tens and ones, and has a picture of the number of counting areas to be used (the divisor).

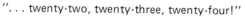

"... twenty-two, twenty-three, twenty-four!"

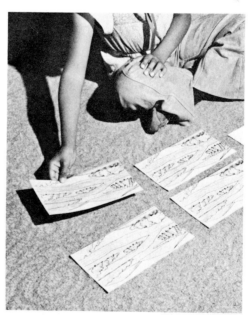

"Divided by four...."

"... puts six on each one! That's twenty-four divided by four equals six."

Cleaning up.

"I'll try another."

PART V

Appendix

Illustrated Glossary of All Materials Needed

The lists and pictures here are included to help individual teachers or workshop leaders who are collecting the materials for the twenty activities on their own. The quantity or measurement for each item represents a composite of what is needed to make all twenty activities.

6 ply railroad board (17 pieces, 11″ X 17″, to be cut into 5½″ X 8″ gameboard backgrounds):

2 azure (for aquariums)
2 dark blue (for sandy beaches)
2 yellow (for watermelons)
2 buff (for haunted houses)
2 brown (for ponds)
2 royal blue (for trees)
1 (11″ X 15″) piece (for pincushion floors)

Felt:

6″ X 12″ yellow (fish tails and yolks)
4″ X 12″ orange (fish tails)
3″ X 12″ brown (bacon)
9″ X 12″ light green (leaves)
18″ X 24″ black (haunted houses—scraps used for hair and mustaches for snapshots)
12″ X 18″ red (watermelon slices)
12″ X 18″ blue (ponds)
9″ X 12″ white (watermelon rind and egg whites)
12″ X 12″ pale yellow (frosting)
18″ X 24″ dark green (pine trees—scraps used for strawberry tops)
9″ X 12″ dark green (leaves)

Twenty storage boxes covered in colorful red and blue waterproof, smudge-proof paper.*

Tagboard (75 sheets, 8½" X 11"):

    Gameboards: Chickens
                    Airports
                    Spaghetti
                    Leaves
                    Strawberries
                    Snapshots
                    Birthday Cakes
                    River Rocks

  2 sets of labels for storage boxes
  10 sets of numeral cards
  10 sets of 4 different equation cards (Total: 40)

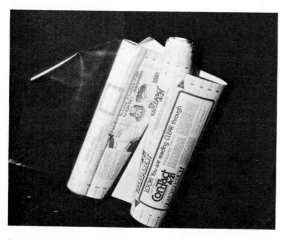

Full roll of clear contact paper* (for protecting
    gameboards, numeral cards and equation cards)

*Individual storage boxes and rolls of clear contact paper
are available separately as a service to teachers from the
Center for Innovation in Education. Write and ask for
current prices and ordering information.

Two pieces of heavy cardboard
    (to be cut into 1¼" X 15 11/16" separator strips:
    1. 12½" X 15 11/16"
    2. 11¼" X 15 11/16"

6 (3 oz.) cans of spray paint:

  Orange (for pumpkins and fish)
  Yellow (for fish and pincushions)
  Red (for strawberries and pincushions)
  Green (for frogs and strawberries)
  Brown (for toads and nests)
  Silver (for airplanes)

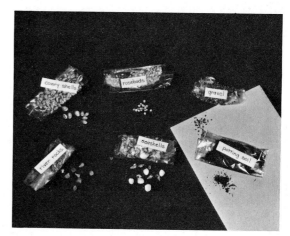

Rocks and shells:

  1/8 cup gravel (for aquarium)
  1/4 cup potting soil (for nes s)
  1/2 cup river rocks
  2/3 cup shells (for sandy beaches)
  1/8 cup rosecup shells (for mouse ears)
  1/2 cup yellow-ringed cowry shells (for mouse
    bodies)

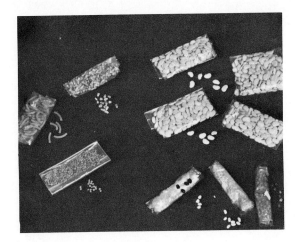

Dry goods:

    3/4 cup large lima beans (for strawberries)

    3/4 cup large lima beans (for fish)

    3/4 cup large lima beans (for pumpkins and ghosts)

    1¼ cup large lima beans (for frogs and toads)

    1/3 cup of corn

    1/8 cup lentils (for frogs' eyes)

    1/2 cup cut macaroni (for spaghetti and meatballs)

    3/4 cup large lima beans (for snapshots)

Treated dry goods:

    1/3 cup red and green spray painted garbanzo beans
    (apples)

    1/4 cup black and white spray-painted baby lima
    beans (watermelon seeds)

    1/4 cup pale yellow and baby blue large navy or
    great northerners (eggs)

Miscellaneous items:

    8 portion cups (for nests)

    8 plastic medicine cups (for buckets)

    4 red pipe cleaners (for buckets)

    1 yard of 1/2" red ball trim (for meatballs)

    1/2 teaspoon yellow paint and 1/2 cup salt (for
    vanilla cookie dough)

    2 teaspoons brown paint and 1/2 cup salt (for
    chocolate cookie dough)

    2 feet of "crystal" and 2 feet of "tangerine" faceted
    plastic beads (for bulbs on the trees)

    10 packages of Stimudents (for airplanes)

    2 wheels of beaded pins (for pincushions)

    2" X 12" pieces of foam (for pincushions)

    16 paper plates (for cookies and bacon and eggs)

    8 (8") lengths of wire (mousetraps)

    8 (3" X 5") pieces of plywood (mousetraps)

    2 sheets (8" X 10") sandpaper

    8 heavy duty rubber bands (mousetraps)

    20 large heavy duty rubber bands (for securing lids
    of storage boxes)

    2 boxes of candles (for birthday cakes)

    32 library pockets

    1 fine line permanent ink marking pen

    1 yard pink yarn, 1 yard black yarn (for mice)

    1 tube plastic model airplane glue (for mice)

Items supplied by the teacher:

    2 bottles of Elmer's white glue

    Crayons

    X-acto knife or single-edged razor blade (for birth-
    day cakes)

    paper cutter, plyers

    20 paper clips (for securing rubber bands on storage-
    box lids)

    masking tape

    1 cup grass clippings (for nests)

All of the materials pictured in the glossary pages 122–
124 are mailed to teachers as part of Mary Baratta-
Lorton's WORKJOBS II Correspondence Course. For
information on the course please write to:

WORKJOBS II
Center for Innovation in Education
19225 Vineyard Lane
Saratoga, CA 95070

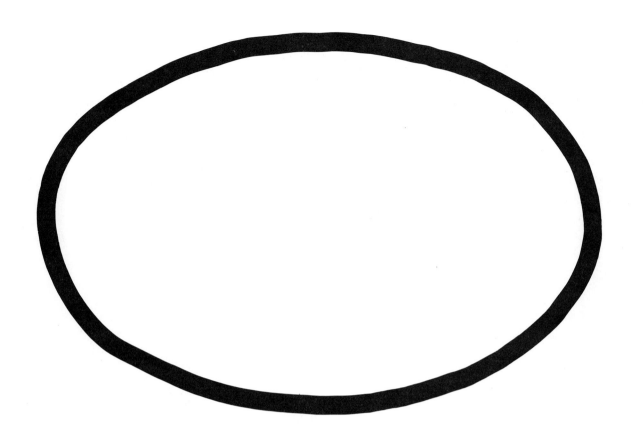

•

_____

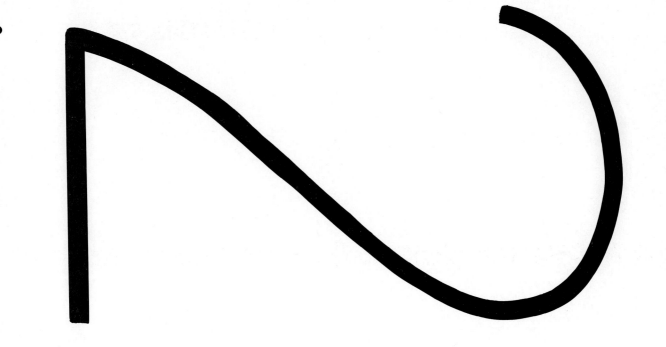

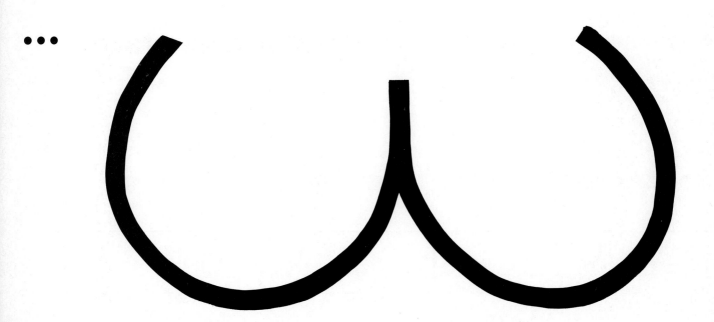

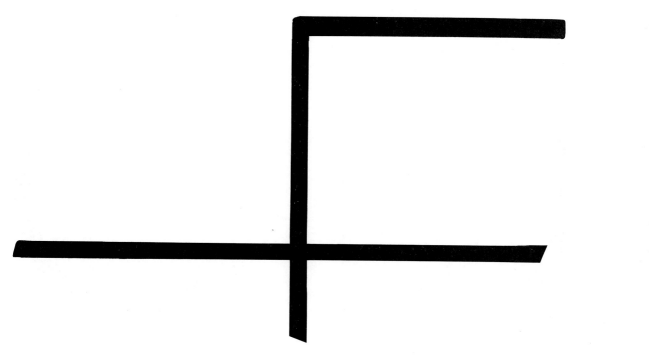

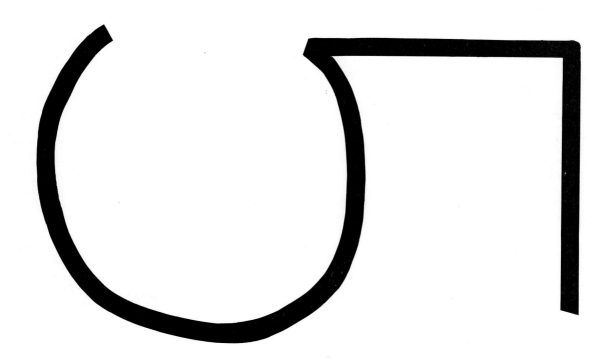

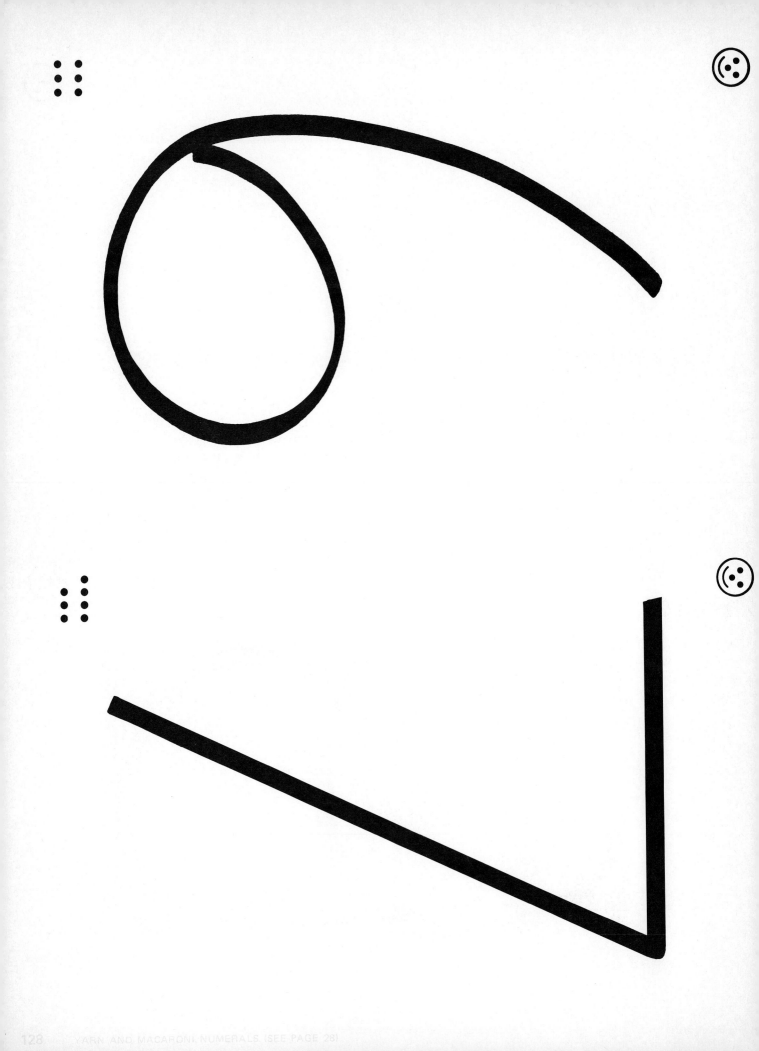

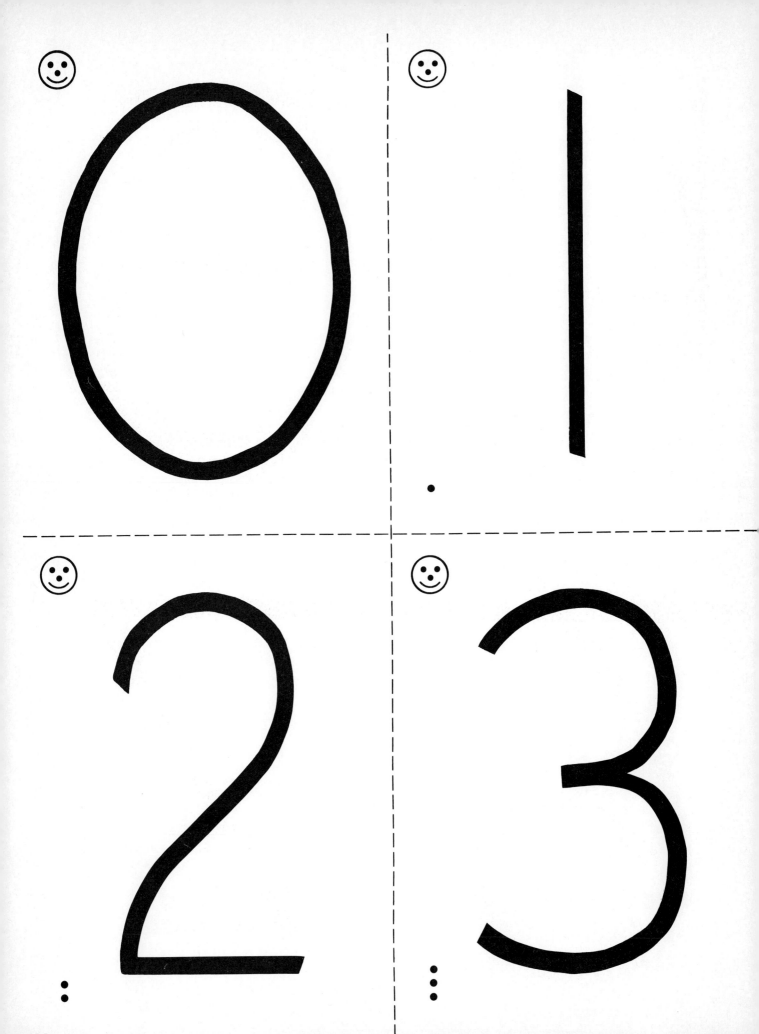

YARN AND MACARONI NUMERALS (SEE PAGE 28)

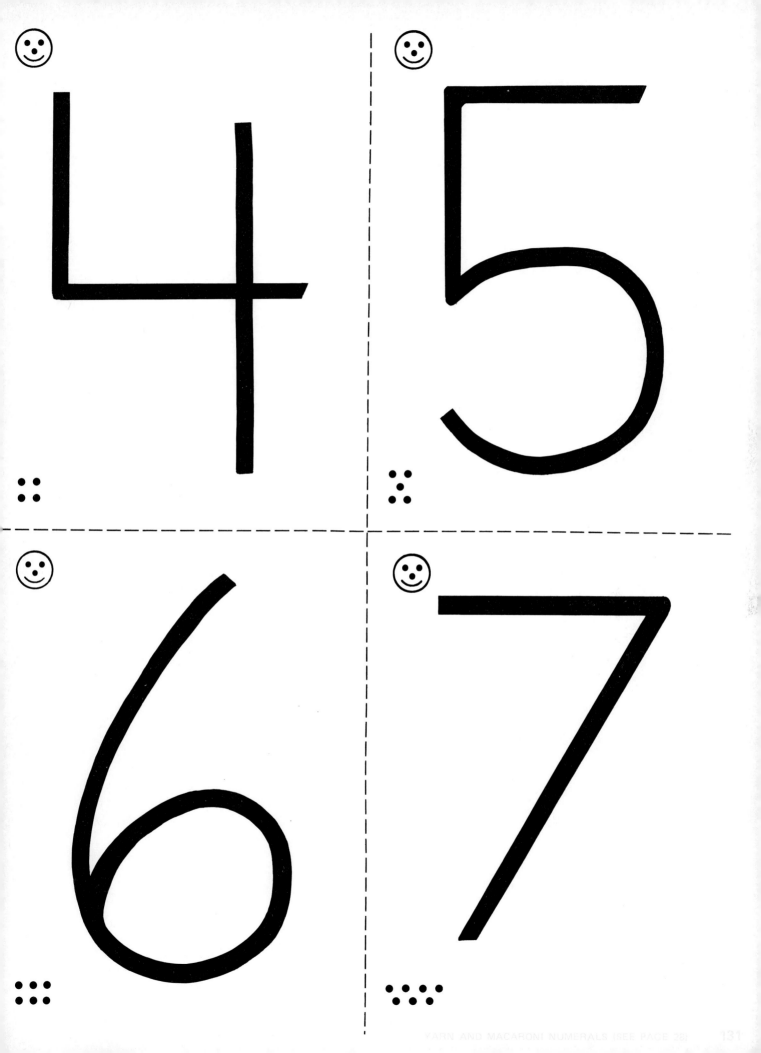

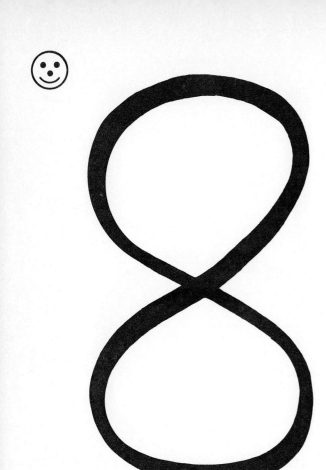

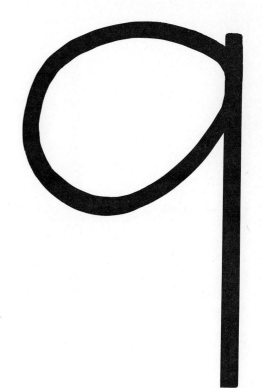

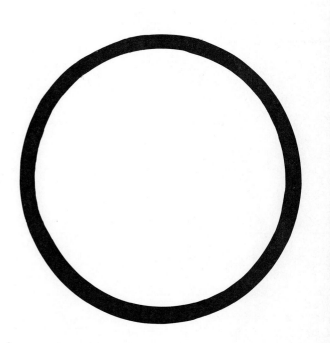

1	aquariums	11	mousetraps
2	nests	12	apples
3	trees	13	leaves
4	pincushions	14	strawberries
5	chickens	15	frogs and toads
6	cookies	16	bacon and eggs
7	airports	17	snapshots
8	watermelon	18	birthday cakes
9	halloween	19	river rocks
10	spaghetti	20	sandy beaches

1	aquariums	11	mousetraps
2	nests	12	apples
3	trees	13	leaves
4	pincushions	14	strawberries
5	chickens	15	frogs and toads
6	cookies	16	bacon and eggs
7	airports	17	snapshots
8	watermelon	18	birthday cakes
9	halloween	19	river rocks
10	spaghetti	20	sandy beaches

0 1 2 3 4

5 6 7 8 9

0 1 2 3 4

5 6 7 8 9

0 1 2 3 4

5 6 7 8 9

2+2	2+4
3+3	3+4
4+4	4+3
5+5	5+2
4+1	2+5
1+5	3+5
2+3	5+3
3+2	5+0
4+2	3+0

5−1	4−3
3−2	4−4
5−0	3−1
4−2	3−0
5−2	5−5
3−3	2−2
4−0	5−3
2−0	2−1
5−4	4−1

EASIER SUBTRACTION (SEE PAGE 105)

6+1	2+8
1+7	8+2
8+1	3+6
9+1	6+3
1+9	7+3
2+6	3+7
6+2	5+5
2+7	4+6
7+2	6+4

6−3	9−5
8−5	7−0
7−7	8−2
9−2	9−8
7−2	7−5
8−0	6−4
9−7	8−8
6−1	6−6
8−6	9−6

LEAVES AND AIRPORTS GAMEBOARDS (SEE PAGES 73 AND 55)

HAPPY BIRTHDAY

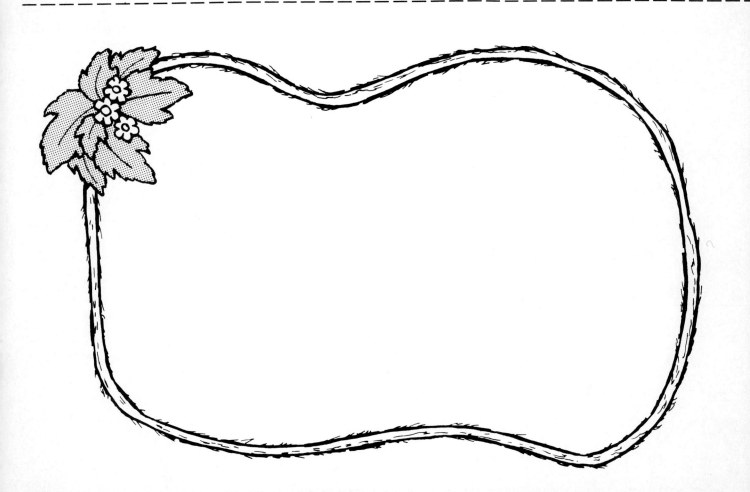

Trace or Xerox these patterns so as to keep the page intact.

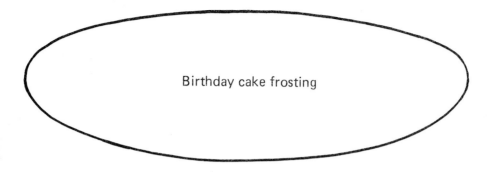

Birthday cake frosting

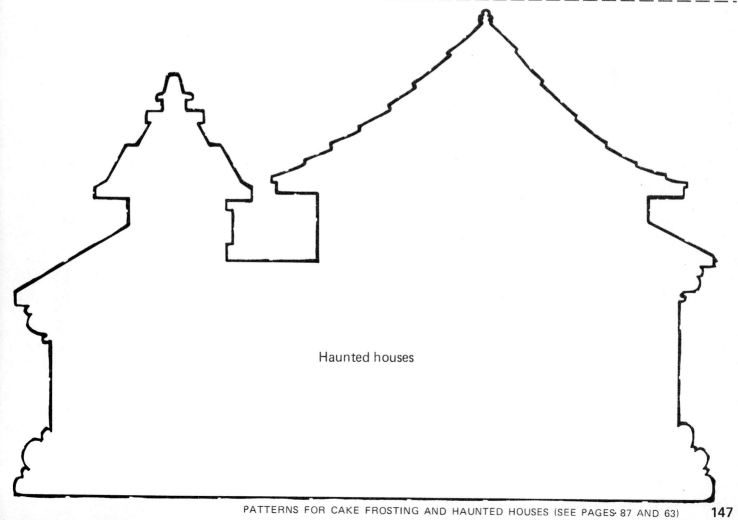

Haunted houses

Trace or Xerox these patterns so as to keep the page intact.

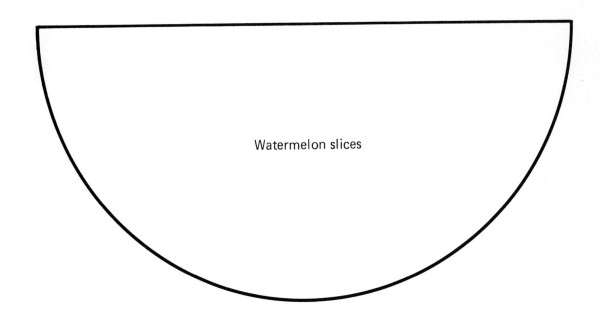

Watermelon slices

Trees

Make a copy of each template. Use the copy to mark half of the felt, then flip the template over to mark the other half.

Egg white template

Flip ↓

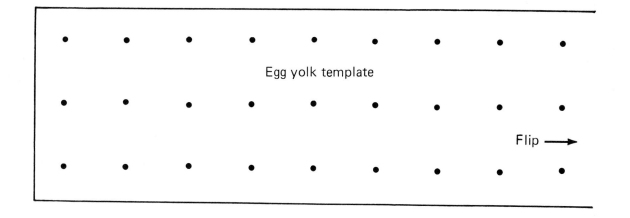

Egg yolk template

Flip ⟶

My Tiny
Number
Book

My Tiny
Number
Book

My Tiny
Number
Book

My Tiny
Number
Book

My Tiny
Number
Book

My Tiny
Number
Book

My Tiny
Number
Book

My Tiny
Number
Book

My Tiny
Number
Book

My Tiny
Number
Book

My Tiny
Number
Book

My Tiny
Number
Book

My Tiny
Number
Book

My Tiny
Number
Book

My Tiny
Number
Book

My Tiny
Number
Book

My Tiny
Number
Book

My Tiny
Number
Book

My Tiny
Number
Book

My Tiny
Number
Book

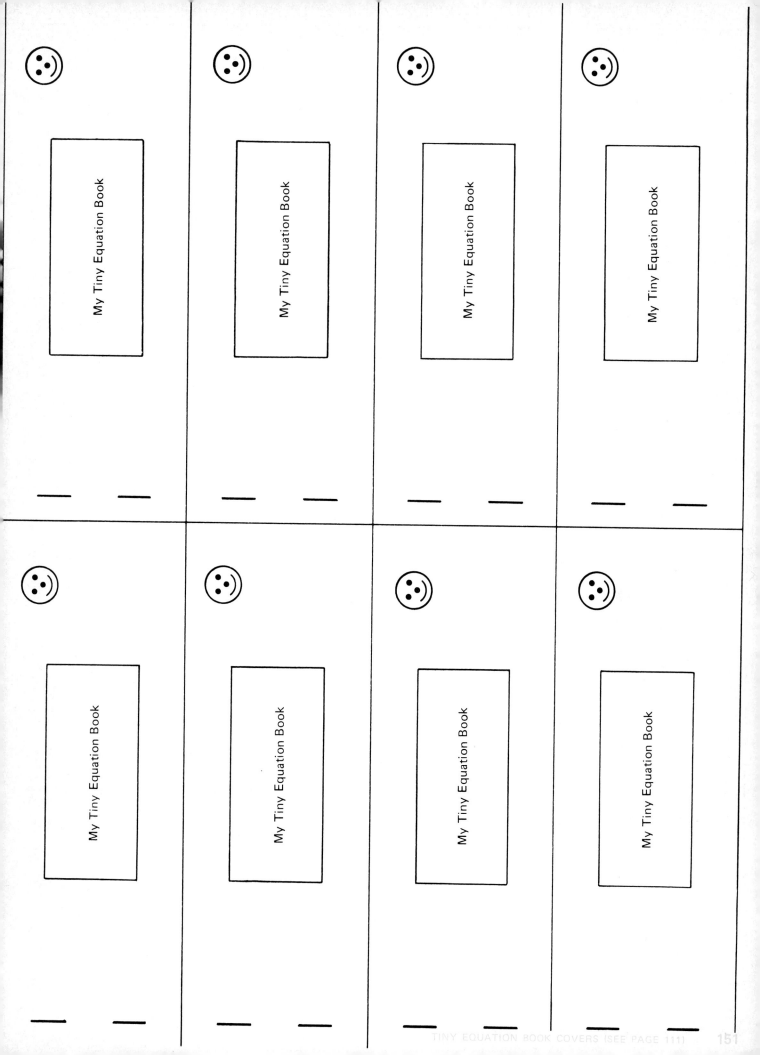

My Tiny Equation Book

My Tiny Equation Book

My Tiny Equation Book

My Tiny Equation Book

My Tiny Equation Book

My Tiny Equation Book

My Tiny Equation Book

My Tiny Equation Book

4

3

2

1

5

7

6

9

8

0

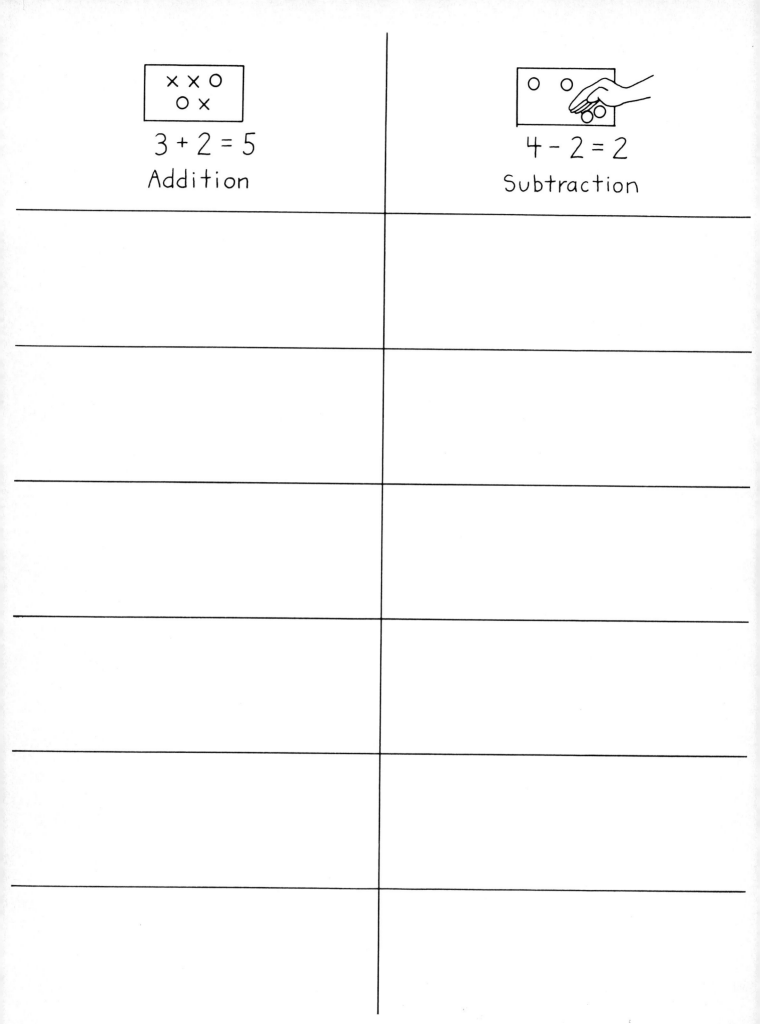

$3 + 2 = 5$

Addition

$4 - 2 = 2$

Subtraction